Divine Healing Power
Today's Greatest Hope

Dr. Jean-Marie Sumo

Primix Publishing
11620 Wilshire Blvd
Suite 900, West Wilshire Center, Los Angeles, CA, 90025
www.primixpublishing.com
Phone: 1-800-538-5788

© 2024 Dr. Jean-Marie Sumo. All rights reserved.
Sumo Publishing Int'l
Fax: 1-866-902-4718
www.sumopublishers.com

All Rights Reserved.
No part of this book may be reproduced, stored in a retrieval system, or transmitted by any means without the written permission of the author. Brief excerpts may be used with the permission of the author for purposes of media reviews.

All quotations are taken from the following Versions of the HOLY BIBLE unless noted otherwise:
New International Version (NIV): Copyright 1973, 1978, 1984 International Bible Society. Used by permission of Zondervan Publishing House. Initials are not noted on NIV quotations.

King James Version (KJV) initials are noted.
New King James Version (NKJV) initials are noted

We have decided not to give importance or respect to satan, to the point of overlooking the grammatical rule of not capitalizing the name.

Published by Primix Publishing: 08/02/2024

ISBN: 979-8-89194-114-4(sc)
ISBN: 979-8-89194-222-6(hc)
ISBN: 979-8-89194-115-1(e)

Library of Congress Control Number: 2024902154

Any people depicted in stock imagery provided by iStock are models, and such images are being used for illustrative purposes only.

Certain stock imagery © iStock.

Because of the dynamic nature of the Internet, any web addresses or links contained in this book may have changed since publication and may no longer be valid. The views expressed in this work are solely those of the author and do not necessarily reflect the views of the publisher, and the publisher hereby disclaims any responsibility for them.

To my Lord and Savior, Yeshua Hamashiach, who brought me out of the darkness of ignorance into his marvelous light and to the place where I could and can still experience the grace of the revelation of his knowledge, the sharing of his suffering, and the power of his resurrection. I recognize my Lord and Savior, Yeshua Hamashiach, as the giver of life, the healer of mankind, and the deliverer of the oppressed. He is the husband of the widow and the father of the parentless. He graciously called me by name to serve him.

The Lord placed on my heart to write this book because he knew this would be a blessing for many people. To him alone be the glory and honor forever and ever. Amen.

Endorsement

Pastor Jean-Marie Sumo is an amazing man of God. From the first moment we met, I sensed something special about him and his wife. Their passion for Christ was so obvious in their worship and in the worship of their children, but, beyond that, there was an expression of faith and hope that far exceeded any I had seen previously. His commitment to serving God through proclamation and obedience is most seen in his testimony, writings, and preaching on the subject of healing. His own experiences have caused him to challenge the body of Christ to dig deep in their faith to believe in Christ, not only as Savior and Deliverer, but as Healer. This well-written book will challenge readers to greater faith in the power of Christ and hopefully serve to deliver some from an overdependence on medications and drugs that are sometimes unnecessary and only serve to mask the symptoms. Sumo doesn't deny great strides made in medical science, but he certainly cautions us on using it as a total replacement to a deep faith in the Lord. I, like him, yearn to see God's miraculous power move in an unprecedented way.

Reverend Bill Roberts
Pastor, Christ Chapel Church
Woodbridge, Virginia

Pastor Sumo gives new meaning to the phrase "out of Africa" with his anointed book, *Divine Healing Power*, which brings Messiah's heritage of healing to the church in America. He shares a biblical truth about the Living God bringing his virtuous healing and baptism of fire to the wounded and broken church. Moreover, he brings the manifestation of fire and how to walk in the redemptive healing power of Messiah in today's world. This book is a must read for all believers wishing to walk in God's promises of divine healing power.

Nona Cash
Leaves of the Olive Tree Ministries
Acworth, Georgia

Table of Contents

Acknowledgments xi
Foreword xv
Introduction 1

Part I The Problem of Health in Human Society

Today's Greatest Hope 9
Different Aspects of the Scientific Health Research 13
The Problem of Wrong Medication 19
Biblical Experiences 27

Part II Origin of Diseases and the Curses

The Different Categories of Mankind Curses 41
The Divine Maledictions: Curses Pronounced by God 45
Cursed Is the Ground 55
You Are Under a Curse 61
Salvation from the Flood 65
The Curse of Noah 71
The Curses of the Law 77
Importance of Blessing versus Cursing 81

Part III Spiritual Warfare

Satan and Demons Are Real 87

Who Is Satan?......................................95
Spiritual Warfare..................................105

Part IV The Solution and Testimony Of Yeshua Hamashiach

God's Promise for Health and Healing 115
The Healing Promise Fulfilled........................125
Yeshua Hamashiach Is the Solution....................129
The Testimony of the Lord Yeshua Hamashiach 137
Exhortation......................................171
About the Author................................. 177

Acknowledgments

I thank God for blessing me with a wonderful family. My wife, Elizabeth Sumo, is a mighty testimony of divine healing power. I thank and glorify the Lord for your life. The best is yet to come because your story has already edified many women and families, and will continue to do so as long as this book is read and for the glory of God.

To my children, Elisha R. Sumo, Elizabeth M. Sumo, Jean-Marie Sumo Jr., and Patrice A. Sumo, you are my crown and glory and a gift God has placed in my life. I want you to know that you have brought me joy and filled my heart with a love that can only come from God. I rejoiced at your birth and have continued to rejoice to this day.

To my brothers, Pierre Adrien Sumo, Saint Germes Emile, Honoré François Sumo, Isaac Sumo, Henry F. Sumo, Eugene (late), and Jean Daniel Sumo, and my only beloved sister, Marie Caroline,

I thank the Lord for all of you and for your love and support for one another. You all are very special.

To the Robinson family, brother in Christ Minister Alfred, I want to acknowledge you and thank you from the bottom of my heart. You and your family opened your door to my wife and I when we came to the United States as missionaries, and made your home available to start this ministry. Thank you.

To the woman of God Betty Nana Coleman, a vessel that God has used to uplift my soul and to encourage me and my family, the Lord's grace will multiply in your life.

To my pastors and spiritual mentors, Pastor Jean Remi Dipakayi in Brussels, Belgium; Thomas Ambassa (late) of the Evangelical Church in Cameroon, your teachings and lives have impacted me to this day. Pastor Cedric Kamga (late), I won't omit the man of God who baptized me and led my first steps into the path of faith in the divine power.

To my friends in Kingdom Service; (The late) Archbishop William P. Brown, president and founder of New Day FIG, the writer of the foreword of this book. To Rev. Bill Roberts of Christ Chapel in Virginia, thank you all for your endorsements, and thank you Rev. Roberts, for your participation in my dissertation defense, remembering that in 2008, you stirred me up for my academic decisions

To the loving memory of my parents, Jethro and Elisabeth Sumo (now with the Lord), who raised eight sons and one daughter, setting an example of love and compassion that remained embedded in my heart. The legacy continues.

Finally, I want to mention the nation of Cameroon, the cradle of my childhood. To all those who have been part of my life, who love the Lord and are still laboring in the vineyard. To Christ Disciple Mission Worldwide of Cameroon, all my friends, and relatives, you will always be in my heart and prayers.

God bless all of you, promoters and readers.

Foreword

It brings me great pleasure to introduce Pastor Jean-Marie Sumo and the divine healing power to you. His researched composition is a great health ministry tool for anyone desiring optimum health, regardless of race, religion, or creed. This collaboration of stories and samples is practical, and it will inspire you to reevaluate yourself, physically and spiritually. If you are suffering from various diseases, Pastor Sumo advises you to take time, examine your lifestyle, and ask yourself, "What am I consuming? What do I think about often?" In *Divine Healing Power*, the answers to these questions amazingly give guidance to those seeking deliverance and healing. As the founder and international presiding bishop of the New Day Fellowship of Independent and Global Churches and Ministries, I have known Pastor Sumo for over seven years. His deep sense of sociability in relating with a broad diversity of people reveals a special uniqueness in him. Pastor has attended two conventions held in Chicago and Las Vegas and successfully completed an annual Bishop College and

Leadership Symposium held in April 2005. I've had the privilege of visiting with Pastor and First Lady Sumo in their home, taking notice of their outstanding and welcoming spirit.

As a brother in Christ, Pastor Sumo's teachings have impacted the lives of those who love the Lord Jesus Christ, creating an atmosphere of joy and laughter, which has uplifted saddened souls to empowerment and hope. Pastor Sumo has exhortation and spiritual counseling experience based on the Word of God, which directs those seeking spiritual achievement and physical fullness to get results.

Pastor Sumo has sketched a blueprint from the Word of God for readers to use when seeking the achievement of deliverance and healing for long-term health. A leader, he is very knowledgeable on the subject of spiritual health. He has studied the Word of God in regards to living a disease-free life in distressed times where so many Americans are plagued with ongoing sickness and incurable diseases.

"But don't give up," says Pastor Sumo. *Divine Healing Power* is a solution for readers universally. Pastor Jean-Marie Sumo is a native of Cameroon and pastor to many. He is eagerly ready to expose the root of disease, describe where it originates, and tell how to get the ultimate source of deliverance and healing to those seeking globally. And I believe it is our duty to share good news as we learn about it to our suffering and dying friends, family, and loved ones in Christendom.

After reading *Divine Healing Power*, Pastor Sumo advises readers to continue to study, take immediate actions, and make these practical teachings for deliverance from sickness, causing new choice habits to form for balanced living in the mind, body, and spirit.

In closing, I personally recommend *Divine Healing Power* for pastors and church leaders alike to teach members how to defeat oppositions in the way that gains personal richness and physical wellness.

Archbishop William (Eusebuis) Brown, PhD
International Presiding
Bishop New Day FIG,
Memphis, TN

Introduction

I am writing this book under the complete guidance of Ruach Kodesh (Holy Spirit), our Leader, Teacher, and Comforter.

The content here is trustworthy and true. Every assertion and demonstration is sustained by the Word of God to assure you that, if you believe the Bible, you will be happy to experience the manifestation of the divine healing power in your life for salvation, restoration, or more edification for the saved ones because the Word of God is quick and effective.

When I got saved, I experienced an extraordinary transformation, as well physically as spiritually and emotionally. In my eagerness to understand the manifestation of God's power for our healing and restoration, I sought the Lord in diligent prayers. My desire to know Him in the fullness of His nature and attributes led me to dig into the mystery of a Bible verse. John 4:22, "…for salvation is from the Jews." It is well known that Yeshua was a Hebrew. The Torah (first five books of the Scriptures) was given to the Hebrews, God's chosen people. Exodus 3:7 says, "…I have indeed seen the misery of my people in Egypt…"

God introduced Himself as the God of the Fathers of the Hebrew people. Exodus 3:14-15, "God said to Moses, "I am who I am. This is what you are to say to the Israelites: I am has sent me to you". God also said to Moses, " Say to the Israelites, the Lord, the God of your fathers – the God of Abraham, the God of Isaac and the God of Jacob – has sent me to you. This is my name forever, the name by which I am to be remembered from generation to generation." All the prophets of the Old Testament as well as the Apostles of the New Testament were Hebrews. I thought there must be something peculiar between God and the Hebrew people. Why did the Lord say to the twelve: Mark 4:11, "He said to them, "To you it has been given to know the mystery of the Kingdom of God; but to those who are outside, all things come in parables," (NKJV).

I undertook a serious research of the roots of the Savior of mankind, not just through the study of my English and French Bibles, but more by inquiries and investigations on the Hebraic culture and ancient traditions. God is good and His love is wonderful. He knew my heart and saw my eagerness to share the extraordinary revelation of healing and restoration power in the name of His Son Yeshua. His Holy Spirit graciously guided me throughout my research.

I emphatically encourage the reader to rely totally upon the veracity of the Word of God in view of its tremendous blessings of restoration, soul, spirit, and body. This will help build up or increase your faith in God and in the power of his Word.

Therefore, since believing or having faith "comes from hearing the message and the message is heard through the word of Christ" (Rom 10:17), I am certain the testimonies of those who have experienced the healing power in the name of Yeshua the Messiah will intensify your confidence in the Lord God Almighty. Your faith may help you also experience the genuine healing power as Ruach Kodesh (Holy Spirit) of God works in you.

As the title indicates, divine healing power exposes the most serious concern of mankind of all times, the problem of health in human society, and demonstrates that the only true, effective, and complete healing from any disease will occur through the will and power of the Lord God Almighty. The goal we all want to achieve is a deeper understanding of the origin of disease and death as results or consequences of disobedience of Adam and Eve to God's command. Because of this original sin, all men are born sinners.

We learn the enemy number one of man on Earth is satan (this name is purposely written in lower case so not to give respect to the evil one). In fact, he is the orchestration of sin in the world. So I am exposing an exciting teaching on spiritual warfare with a detailed knowledge of satan and his army, his demonic strongholds, and his treacherous plans of destruction. This helps the reader understand the role of the devil in man's daily struggle as the unseen ruler of the present world system, so he or she can take a stand against those evil forces through prayers and faith in the Lord, our battle fighter and healer.

God Is Love

Because he does not want any man to perish, in Ezekiel 18, he repeatedly says he does not take pleasure when the sinner dies, but he does take pleasure when the sinner repents and turns away from his or her wicked ways. Ezekiel 18:23, "Do I take any pleasure in the death of the wicked? Declares the Sovereign; rather, am I not pleased when they turn from their ways and live?" Verse 32 concludes: "For I take no pleasure in the death of anyone, declares the Sovereign Lord. Repent and live." So God truly does not want us to suffer from diseases. He loves us and wants us to be happy, just like any good father who would labor for his children's happiness. Yeshua always said that our joy must be complete. Because of this, he has always given man the opportunity and weapon to destroy diseases, defeat the powers of darkness, and maintain a healthy total man, body, soul, and spirit.

If you hear the voice of the Lord, do not hesitate to open your heart and receive him with all the spiritual and physical effects that follow salvation. When by God's grace you have the opportunity to come to his knowledge, trust in him and seek him with all your heart. It does not matter what your present situation is. Do not give up. Keep searching and knocking. Let this book help you strengthen your hope until you find the solution. The blessing of God is awesome.

I encourage the reader, especially the believer who has relied much more on physical science and worldly wisdom, to approach the throne of grace with full assurance and exercise faith as great as that of the woman who had suffered from constant bleeding for twelve years until she touched Yeshua. Hallelujah! She was instantly healed. So will you be.

Yeshua our Savior said, "The thief does not come except to steal and to kill and to destroy. I have come that they may have life and that they may have it more abundantly," John 10:10 (NKJV).

The solution to health problem I have graciously received by revelation and understanding of the divine mysteries here assures us that there is hope for a better life. We can enjoy it plainly in accordance with the Messiah's own declaration that he came to this world so we may have life and have it more abundantly. If we have been saved by God's grace through faith in the Lord and Savior Yeshua, we ought to believe we are also healed by God's grace through faith in the same healer. Yeshua Hamashiach is the solution. He has fulfilled God's promise for our spiritual and physical restoration. God has reconciled us to himself through the works of the cross. The book ends with a series of faith-building testimonies and personal experience of the Lord's extraordinary visitation. I am exposing just one of many.

Everyone must know that the destroyer of your life, your family, and your children is the devil. He is the unseen manager behind diabetes, ulcer, cancer, stroke, leprosy, heart attacks, mental disturbances, and so forth. In order to destroy the works of satan, The Lord Yeshua has come to rebuild your life and restore that which no physical scientific remedy can restore.

Acts 3:6 says, "In the Name of Jesus Christ of Nazareth, rise up and walk." And the cripple stood up and walked. I also invite you, as you read, to walk in the Spirit toward the desires of your heart. Rise up gradually and walk to Yeshua, focusing your mind and heart upon the healer and restorer of broken walls, the one who has graciously granted us the divine healing power.

Part I
The Problem of Health in Human Society

Today's Greatest Hope

As you begin to journey across these pages, my first and dearest wish for you is that this read will impact your life forever. Go through with hope in your heart that the message herein will help make a difference in all the blessings you are expecting from God. If you have been seeking his face for specific needs, whether spiritual or physical, you will certainly find an answer. Because of your hope, this will become a faith-motivating generator for you in Jesus' powerful name.

In consideration of the case that you do not personally know Yeshua the Messiah (or Jesus Christ) as the Lord and Savior of your life and you are holding this book because you hope you will find some answer to your problem, be it physical, material or spiritual, get a bible on the side, for you are holding a shovel that will help dig into the Scriptures where there are answers to all of mankind's problems. I want your hope to be stirred up until you feel a hunger for God's power. You want to reach the place where the door of your heart shall be widely opened for the

Lord to come in, knowing your heart is very precious to he who is faithful. Your heart is so precious because he came into this world in the body of flesh, suffered at your place, and died for you because he loves you.

Yeshua clearly stated: "Behold, I stand at the door and knock. If anyone hears my voice and opens the door, I will come in to him and dine with him, and he with me". Revelation 3:20, (NKJV). Jesus is standing at the door. This is the door of your and anybody's heart. If you open and invite him in, he will never say no to you. He will enter and dine with you, work with you, and answer your prayers beyond your expectation.

You may already be in Christ, but not fulfilled. You may have problems or desires that you have been praying for and have kept hoping to see a breakthrough and God's physical manifestation of signs and wonders. This tool will clarify your understanding of spiritual things and stir up your faith as you progress toward the goal the Lord has set up for you, as you know he has a plan set up for you beforehand.

God wishes for us to be healthy. We have many blessings at hand. Financial and material blessings are very important for our total fulfillment. The economic recession and household financial problems are rampant nowadays. Family bankruptcies are increasing at a faster rate than ever before. However, I am first emphasizing on hope in the context of divine healing because our healthy condition remains the most envied one of all. My hope is to have and maintain a healthy soul in a healthy body.

Hope generates expectation when it grows to faith, according to the biblical definition given in Heb 11:1 (NKJV). "Now faith is the substance of things hoped for, the evidence of things not seen." The two key words to highlight here are "substance" and "evidence." The literal translation of this same verse from the Louis Second French Bible renders, "Now faith is the firm assurance of things hoped for and the demonstration of those not seen."

Your hope is not faith until you begin to feel a total and peaceful assurance that it is done. You must remain firm in that assurance (that is, no doubt should step in to waver your assurance). Then begin to see the result real with the eye of the Spirit who dwells in you. This is the priority mind-set in prayer and petition to God. Hebrews 11:6 (NKJV) says, "But without faith it is impossible to please Him, for he who comes to God must believe that He is, and that He is a rewarder of those who diligently seek Him."

God takes a lot of pleasure when we trust in Him. The disciples, who walked and ate with the Lord and hugged Him good morning and good night, had to ask Him one day, "Lord, increase our faith." They had understood the importance and deep meaning of what they hoped for, and their faith was to be the generator of the manifestation of God's power in their lives. If those considered as the pillars of the gospel had to ask and almost beg the Lord to increase their faith. After two thousand years should we not be crying to Him even more for faith? Jesus always told those he healed, "Your faith has healed you."

Health has been (and still is) the number one concern of the human race throughout the existence of the world. Every individual's health concern starts from the day he is conceived in the womb and endures during his entire life until he ceases to exist. Elsewhere, the world's largest and highest financial investment of human resources is that of medical science research. One of the most important wishes expressed in the Scriptures is that of being healthy. The third epistle of John verse two says, "Beloved,

I pray that you may proper in all things and be in health, just as your soul prospers."

It is evident that man has been seeking the solution to his health problems everywhere except where the solution is, the Bible. I also hope the Apostle John's prayer will be effective in your life through this read. Let this be a blessing for you and your family, your friends, and your acquaintances.

Different Aspects of the Scientific Health Research

Scientific research in general, the invention of medical equipment, and the persistent experimentation of medication, especially for those painful diseases that cannot be found in the patient's body or cured, have produced tremendous expenses. Research has brought satisfactory results in the areas of natural diseases. "Natural" means they can be seen and touched and their manifestations are palpable. The presence of spiritual beings provokes unknown and unseen diseases. Every attempt to locate and cure them has proved to be of no avail.

We are living in a world system that only deals with the physical environment. It does not seek to comprehend the manifestations in the spiritual realms, so it cannot understand them. In science, we never learned about spiritual beings or "demonic manifestations" in human life. However, God, who has created all things, can reveal their understanding to whoever he chooses to.

It is obvious that the wisdom and knowledge of physical science must be limited before the mysteries of God. God says: It is obvious that the wisdom and knowledge of physical science must be limited before the mysteries of God. God says:

> These people come near to me with their mouth and honor me with their lips, but their hearts are far from me. Their worship of me is made up only of rules taught by men. Therefore once more I will astound these people with wonder upon wonder; the wisdom of the wise will perish, the intelligence of the intelligent will vanish (Isa 29:13–14).

Added to the fact that heaven and earth shall pass away, but the word of God will stand forever, we must acknowledge that human wisdom, which has enabled him to do wonderful works on Earth (science and technology, discoveries, and inventions), became confused before God's splendor, despite all the wonderful scientific inventions and discoveries I commend greatly. Far from despising human science, I am espousing the glorious power of the Creator who brought all things from inexistence to existence with the word.

> No matter the magnitude of human wisdom and knowledge, though theological as it may be, no man can discern the wisdom of the Lord God Almighty unless by the Spirit of God. "We have not received the spirit of the world but the Spirit who is from God, that we may understand what God has freely given us. This is what we speak, not in words taught us by human wisdom but in words taught by the Spirit, expressing spiritual truths

in spiritual words. The man without the Spirit (or the natural man) does not accept the things that come from the Spirit of God, for they are foolishness to him, and he cannot understand them, because they are spiritually discerned. The spiritual man makes judgments about all things, but he himself is not subject to any man's judgment: "For who has known the mind of the Lord that he may instruct Him? But we have the mind of Christ" (1 Cor 2:12–16).

These verses have to be taken into great consideration in order to accept, understand the divine blessings that will flow in your life through this book, and fully receive those blessings. Because the power of God manifested to heal, restore, and strengthen us, this is as available to us as the atmosphere.

God is Spirit. Whoever wants to deal with spiritual matters must enter in communion with him, "have the mind of Christ," for Jesus said, John 4: 24, "God is spirit, and his worshipers must worship in spirit and in truth. There are many "worshipers" on Earth, but very few even understand what "in spirit and in truth" means. Nearly all of Jesus Christ's believers in this world today think they are worshipping God just because they are told or grew up going to church every Sunday. But, at the same time, the same people complain about spiritual disturbances that are not supposed to be experienced in the life of spirit-filled, born-again persons.

It is sad to live in the midst of such a variety of paradoxical doctrines that have created total confusion in the believer's mind and produced complete skepticism as far as the divine healing power in the mighty sweet name of Jesus Christ is concerned.

It is important to understand that, when I talk about the

Spirit, it is not a matter of being devoted members of any religious institution or a good churchgoer. It is to fully dwell in the glory of God.

In John 17, Jesus said to his father in his powerful prayer of intercession, "I have given them the glory that you gave me."

The church of the Living God is the most powerful clinic ever encountered where the only one supreme doctor and surgeon is Jesus Christ of Nazareth and the generator of the healing power is the Holy Spirit. Glory to God! I must be specific in that it is not a counterfeit church, but the true powerful church of Jesus Christ.

My aim is not to discourage scientific research or medical improvement, which I commend once more. I am aware of the wonderful advancement of medical technology and discoveries in the last century. I consider the remarkable decrease of infant mortality and increase of the average life span everywhere in the world today. I wish God himself would open the understanding of whoever reads these lines to perceive the mystery of the divine healing power. The Holy Spirit will help you dwell in God's power and receive his blessings. Then you will share those blessings with friends and neighbors who are bound by various infirmities in their bodies and hearts.

Despite the great and commendable endeavor of physical medical science in general, mankind is still counting a great number of diseases and plagues that are beyond the human capacity of understanding. Many pains are still totally beyond scientific knowledge. For this reason, research will never cease. Whereas science deals with the natural, physical, and touchable matters, the divine healing power deals with metaphysical or spiritual problems as well as the natural, physical, and touchable problems. Unclean spirits, directly or indirectly, provoke many pains in our bodies. These spirits cannot be seen on an x-ray or microscope slide. Many scientists do not even believe in the existence of those spirits. However, the pains they generate are often subjects of a lot of research.

But here is a research tool that would take any body to the right place for the right answer. The four Gospels of Jesus (Matthew, Mark, Luke, and John) are full of healing and deliverance situations. Jesus gave a remarkable answer to the people that John the Baptist had sent to him. Jesus replied: "Go back and report to John what you hear and see: The blind are receiving sight, the lame walk, those who have leprosy are cured, the deaf hear, the dead are raised, and the good news is preached to the poor" (Matt 11:4).The word of God is quick and powerful. It is sharper than any double-edged sword. It goes into joints and marrow and even divides soul and spirit.

The Word was made flesh and came to dwell among men. He humbled himself onto death and the death of the cross. This is why he was given a name above every name, Jesus Christ. He is the Son of the Living God. Know that, at the name of Jesus, every knee will bow in heaven, on Earth, and under Earth. Every tongue shall confess that Jesus Christ is Lord to the glory of God the Father. The healing power is in that mighty name. The word of God stood in front of a tomb and spoke to the dead, and the tomb released the man alive. What an extraordinary dynamic effect produced from the word of the mouth. "In the beginning was the Word, and the Word was with God, and the Word was God." John 1:1. This is a well-known biblical verse. Physical (or natural) and social problems can be treated with physical remedies that are visible and touchable. But spiritual troubles and even physical as well should be treated with spiritual means. There is no flexibility about this assertion.

How then can anyone dare to imagine that human intelligence or faculty or physical studies would understand those wonders? They are mysteries to us. I am talking here about everybody. Whether you are a Christian or not, believer, or atheist, the divine healing power, as Jesus is sending its report to John above, is a mystery and will remain one until Jesus chooses to reveal it to you. In Matt 11: 25, it says, "At that time Jesus said: 'I praise you Father, Lord of heaven and earth, because you have hidden these thing from the wise and learned, and revealed them to the children". The understanding of the manifestation of the Word into substance is purely revelation. I will talk more about the mystery revealed further.

The good news is that he shed his precious blood for this purpose, that whoever believes in him should not perish. In other words, they should not even go through conditions that lead to perish. "Surely, he took up our infirmities and carried our sorrows,... and by his wound, we are healed." Isaiah 53:4-5. Take serious note of this prophetic and powerful declaration of Isaiah.

The very reason why the Lord laid on my heart to write this book is to share the testimony of Jesus Christ in my life and ministry and work with you, the reader, who needs that same blessing and make you a source of the same to many others. Again, the precious and healing blood of Jesus is fully available to whosoever believes.

The Problem of Wrong Medication

Many diseases and pains originate from and are controlled by unseen forces that human strength cannot master because they are unseen in the physical domain. Spiritual beings generate and manage them, and no sophisticated equipment can locate them.

Every medication is powerless before these unseen beings. Most of the time, the excessive absorption of the medication administered to hopefully stop pains from unknown diseases has caused more harm to the patients than their deliverance.

All the harm caused by drugs or absorption of the medication is referred to as "side effects." The side effects from overtaking drugs cannot be neglected. Physicians themselves warn their patients of those effects.

The purpose of this demonstration is not to stop a sick reader from taking medication. They are helpful as long as they can kill the pain every six to twelve hours and calm the illness gradually until eventual complete relief occurs. My purpose is to challenge the reader to greater faith in the healing power of God, the creator of man.

Unknown diseases have always been opportunities for new experimentation in the research domain. In my divine duty of intercessor, I met sick people who consumed a lot of medication for pains they could not explain. Nor could the physician locate or determine the illness or its causes. But the effects were there, and the patients were suffering enormously. These patients allow the medical research community to experiment with new drugs and medicine.

A typical case about my mother is astonishing. I received a phone call that she was at the hospital, almost dying. According to the medical diagnosis, one doctor said she had Parkinson's disease. Another doctor said she was developing a madness trauma. The quantity of drugs she was administered began to cause other damages in her head, to the point she began not to recognize her children. For days, my wife and I prayed for her over the phone. We kept telling her to trust in the Lord and she would be healed. I challenged her that, not only she would recover, but she would take a trip to the United States and spend some time with us. My mother calls me "Pastor." She said, "Pastor, are you sure I will see you again?" "Oh, yes," I said. Then she said, "Send me the ticket." At that moment, she had faith. Her desire to see us again exploded in her heart.

One of my brothers who lives in France heard about the complicated health issue. He flew home with his personal doctor. At their arrival, the doctor took a few hours to diagnose the problem. My mother had a strong fever, and all she needed was a fever reducer/pain reliever. He took her off all the drugs except the fever tablets. Three days later, my mother was home, eating, drinking, and saying good-bye to her new doctor from Paris.

Six months later, my mother flew to Washington DC and spent a couple months with her grandchildren, enjoying her rest as she never did before. Today, she continues to serve the Lord in her church, having more strength than before. I believe God heard and answered our prayers, and he sent a medical authority to get her away from Parkinson's disease and madness drugs.

A friend of mine, an international businessman, came to me in my church. He brought his mother, who had been in great pain for several years. He told me he had just spent more than sixty thousand dollars during the past seven months, running from one hospital to another, just for medical checkups to find the cause of his mother's suffering.

My friend told me that, according to the medical reports, his mother was in perfect health. Her last examiner suggested she had some psychological disturbance, similar to mental illness, because it was thought she was pretending she had pains. Others thought she had lost her mind and was just crazy enough to feel some pains. Amazingly, even though they could not determine what was wrong, she already had boxes full of prescription medication, costing her over thirty thousand dollars in less than six months. And, while he was trying to explain the whole situation, his mother was lying on the floor, looking halfway dead and groaning in a way that could break your heart. My friend said he had brought his mother here for prayer as a last chance. It was about eight o'clock in the evening while I was waiting for the church intercessors to get in for our regular evening prayer.

I looked at the woman for a while. I turned to talk to my

friend. Right away, the Holy Spirit said to me that demonic forces, operating by witchcraft powers all the way from Africa, had bound the woman.

Countless cases like this are all over the world. My friend said it was true. He proceeded to tell me a long story about his family, and he described the terrible attacks that took place against his own life when he was sixteen years old. When we started the prayer, we drove out the demons from the woman. About ten minutes after we had driven out the demons, we had her sit on a chair. I signaled we should start praise and worship. As we began to sing praise with music and battle shouts, the woman, who was dying earlier, stood up and danced with all her strength, Jumping in the midst of the singing group, she shouted, "Thank you, Jesus! Thank you, Jesus!" She was delivered. To God be the glory, for all the mighty works He has done!

My friend's mother was completely healed. She refused to go back with her son, saying she had found a home with us. She left the church after a week, feeling in good shape.

I traveled to Chicago, IL in August 1997 with my family to visit Manu and Carole, who had been tremendously blessed through the divine healing power. In June 1992, I had visited and preached at the First Haitian Baptist Church of Evanston, where they were attending. At the end of the message, as I went to sit down, the church's pastor, Reverend Gabeau asked me to pray for the sick. More than half of the audience hastened, each one trying to get first to the altar call. Because I had to catch my flight that same afternoon, I did not spend much time praying over each individual. I walked through the crowd, just touching them and saying repeatedly, "Jesus has healed you" or "By the stripes of the Lord Jesus Christ, receive your healing in

Jesus' name." Among that crowd was a lady named Carole. She had been barren for the past twelve years and been healed from a physically unknown sickness. Later that year, she conceived five babies at the same time. Many others were also healed from tuberculosis, diabetes, and various pains. The Lord performed signs and wonders in that church as a revival broke out of there.

The man with tuberculosis was an invitee who had heard about this special service when it had been announced on the radio that morning. He accepted Jesus Christ as his Savior and Lord of his life. Four years later, he was serving on the Deacon Board.

Thank God for what he did for Carole and her family. Her system could not sustain five children, but God allowed three to come out alive. They are healthy and strong today. When I heard about this wonderful testimony of the Lord Jesus Christ operating through my humble hand, I decided to see the little children. So I traveled from Washington DC to Chicago with my family in July 1997. Pastor Gabeau took that opportunity to set up a one-week revival program.

Carole and her husband, Manu, also invited many friends and colleagues who had heard or known about her testimony to see us and pray with us. Among those friends, a particular case drew my attention. Colette had a twelve-year-old daughter in the hospital who had been declared clinically dead for many days. She was simply dead, but still under the machines.

The medical team in charge was waiting for the mother, urging her to authorize the disconnection of the machines. When she told me her whole problem, the Holy Spirit revealed to me that sorcerers had sold the child's soul to the voodoo powers of darkness. We were dealing here with a combination on Haitian voodoo and high-level witchcraft operating from West Africa.

Spirits have no frontier, border, or respect for immigration laws. In the physical, her daughter's pain could not be located. Nor the illness could be found. Unfortunately, she had taken so much medication that her blood was damaged. The little girl had died from the overdose of medicines that could not even have any effect on witchcraft powers. We went to the hospital the following day. After I read Isa 61 and Ps 23 to the girl and began to pray the sinner's prayer that leads to receiving Christ the Savior, she opened her eyes slightly, and tears ran down. She closed back her eyes and went away in peace. I told Colette that, even on her deathbed, the merciful Lord brought her baby from the deepest gloom into paradise. Colette's forty-year-old sister, Nancy, gained over two hundred pounds within a few months due to excessive medication for unknown diseases in her body. When I prayed for her in June 1998, I told her to stop destroying herself with unnecessary medication and begin to take the tablets of God. In other words, call on the healing presence of the Almighty God.

Some of the pains left her body, but she did not obey my instructions. She kept suffering from something that her physician had called by an invented name. A year later, I visited the family again. Nancy was almost twice bigger than before, and her health condition was worse.

I advised her again, giving her the Word through the Scriptures. This time, she obeyed my instructions and accepted Jesus Christ as her Lord and Savior. She was completely delivered from unclean spirits. That evening, we had a wonderful night prayer service in that house.

At the time I am beginning to write this spiritual guide for divine healing in January 1999, she is enjoying perfect health, and her weight is going down gradually.

One month after this visit, Colette and her family took a flight from Chicago to Washington DC to my church, where they spent almost a week under intensive prayers of deliverance. Men and women of God joined prayers and forces together to sustain this family in warfare against voodoo organizations. The good part in this battle is that Jesus Christ is the healer and deliverer. We pray on Earth, and he is the one who destroys the works of darkness in the spiritual realms. We just did our part in obedience to his commands. Because he is faithful and true, by his stripes, we receive healing deliverance and blessings.

They went back to Chicago extremely happy. Now Sister Colette's entire household is enjoying good health and happiness in the Lord. They also made their home a house of prayer. Glory to God!

I just want every believer who acknowledges there is power in the blood of Jesus to reconsider his or her faith and pray. Ask God for individual revival and spiritual breakthrough. You will gain victory over the devil and his witchcraft organizations. Don't just be lying down under machines that will never have an effect on spirits. Those who desire effective healing should believe that "... God exists and that He rewards those who earnestly seek Him". Hebrews 11:6

Biblical Experiences

As a spiritual counselor, I have experienced many extraordinary physical effects of restoration while dealing with spiritual matters. We understand the physical body is the temple of the Holy Spirit. Therefore, if the Holy Spirit lives in this temple, this temple must be pure and holy. It says in 3 John 2, "Dear friends, I pray that you may enjoy good health and that all may go well with you, even as your soul is getting along well."

So, if your soul is getting along well and if you are spiritually healthy, the temple that shelters this healthy soul should be healthy as well. I am convinced this is not a way of thinking. It is a fact. The indwelling Holy Spirit works wonders sometimes when we are not aware of it. Jesus did promise to the disciples, including you and me, that they would receive power as a result of receiving the Holy Spirit.

I have seen people being healed or just relieved from pain while we were talking. For example, during a church service, Gigi, a visitor, spoke with me for less than ten minutes before the congregation. After the service was over, she came to me and testified that serious pain had left her body, shouting in great amazement, "You have the healing power!"

We did not speak about her pain or healing. She had not told me that she had an accident and her elbow and arm were presenting some infirmities. I did not pray either.

We spoke about Jesus. She expressed a great curiosity to know him. And Jesus, who was right there, touched her. The divine healing power flew upon the woman. And she was healed instantly.

The Bible clearly shows us the source, operation, and result of the divine healing power in both the Old and New Testaments. As far as our salvation is concerned, there is only one name that has been given to the world through which we have known the grace to be saved, Yeshua Hamashiach of Nazareth, the Son of the Living God. He is the anointed one who is able to break the yoke and free us from bondage.

He is also the one that was spoken about by the Spirit of the Lord God Almighty through the prophet saying, "By his stripes, we are healed."

The story of Naaman (2 King 5) recalls an extraordinary manifestation of the healing power through the instruction of the prophet of God. Naaman was commander of the army of the king of Aram. He was a great man in the sight of his king because, through him, God had given victory to him. But, Naaman, although he was a valiant soldier, had leprosy. He heard about the man of God in Israel, the man through whom the Lord was displaying his glorious power. He traveled from his country to Jerusalem to meet the king for authorization to consult the man of God. When he arrived at his final destination, Elisha, the prophet of God, did not even rush out to welcome the commander of the army of Aram. He sent his servant to tell him to dip himself into the Jordan River seven times.

> Naaman became angry and left. As he was on his way back, his servant went to him and said: My father, if the prophet had told you to do some great thing, would you not have done it? How much more, then, when he tells you, "Wash and be cleansed." So he went down and dipped himself in the Jordan seven times, as the man of God had told him, and his flesh was restored and became clean like that of a young boy (2 King 5:13–14).

This is amazing. Now, if this happened to Naaman, it will happen to you as well. God displayed his glory through the word of his prophet. And, because Naaman finally obeyed the prophet's instructions, he was blessed as he experienced the divine healing power.

The God of Elisha is exactly the same God we serve today. He is sitting on the same throne of glory, pouring down the same love and blessing over those who fear him. Nehemiah 1:5 says, "Love him and obey his commands."

About six hundred years before Christ, the Prophet Isaiah said, "By his stripes, we are healed" (Isaiah 53:5, NKJV). Now the prophet spoke in the present tense, showing that, before the Lord Jesus Christ came on Earth in the body of flesh to suffer and die for sinners, he was already healing those who believed in his word through his prophets.

> I would like to warn the reader once more about prophets or men of God. Just as in the days of Isaiah and

Jeremiah, many false prophets were leading the people of God astray. In Acts 20:29– 30, it says: "savage wolves will come in among you and will not spare the flock. Even from your own number men will arise and distort the truth in order to draw away disciples after them."

I wish you to have the spirit of discernment to avoid falling into the trap of the devil, like Adam and Eve, who despised God's commands to believe the devil's lies. For instance, 2 Cor. 11:13 says: "For such men are false apostles, deceitful workers, transforming themselves into the apostles of Christ. And no wonder for satan himself is transformed into an angel of light. It is not surprising, then, if his ministers also be transformed as the ministers of righteousness. Their end will be what their actions deserve".

We are living in a time when faith in divine healing among the believers has surrendered to total trust to physicians and medications. Believing in divine healing and receiving complete healing and/or deliverance from evil strongholds is extremely scarce in our churches today. The devil has unfortunately succeeded in turning the hearts of church people from the Living Word to the full trust in their doctors and medication. Most of the time, the power of drugs is to numb the body or part of the body that is in pain, at least for just a little time. That is why the drugs are to be administered in a regular manner for days, weeks, or entire lifetime. There is no medication to make a paralytic walk because we demonstrate by the Scriptures that the paralyzed is in demonic bondage. But in the name of Yeshua, the demon that has bound the legs will loose and flee, and the cripple will stand and walk. That's the Bible.

With God, you will get exactly what you believe in. You cannot mix the physical science healing with divine operation. In Isaiah 42:8, God said, "I am the Lord; that is my name! I will not give my glory to another or my praise to idols". He alone has to take all the glory and honor because he has all the power to heal. So there is a choice for any individual who comes to God for healing. You count on God and place your faith in him alone, or you count on science, stick with it, and have total faith in it. Experience has shown that both do not work together. Psalm 62:5-8, "My soul, wait silently for God alone, for my expectation is from Him. He only is my rock and my salvation; He is my defense; I shall not be moved. In God is my salvation and my glory; the rock of my strength, and my refuge, is in God. Trust in Him at all times, you people;..." (NKJV)

Somebody said to me one day, "Pastor Sumo, this is too hard to comprehend. You know we live in a time of scientific advancement." I told him, "You're right. Don't get me wrong. I am not against science or medical improvement of this age. My concern is the level of faith in divine healing in the church today. There are more incurable diseases like cancer, diabetes, heart attack, kidney failure, and more in the midst of the Christian people than in the secular world, right?" He said, "Yes."

I said, "Why? Because you have put your trust more in your physician than in the divine healer, Christ the Son of God, in whom you believe." He asked me again, "So, if you get sick, won't you go to the hospital or doctor?"

I said, "That's a very pertinent question. I am writing this book because the divine healing is not only trustworthy and true, but it is the testimony of the Lord Yeshua of Nazareth for my life." As long as I abide by the word of the Lord in Exodus 15:26, the Lord shall also and always be; "I am the Lord who heals you." How is it possible to get sick when I know I just have to do my part? What does it require for me to be healthy? God is even more faithful to do his. God has blessed me to be a blessing for a dying people who are supposed to fully trust or have faith in him. Remember that, if you have faith, just like a mustard seed, you will speak to any mountain (sickness, spirit, or even enemy) to get out. Then it will obey. There is no secret about this. Everything is in the Scriptures. People believe in Jesus Christ, go to church, and build or help build fantastic, large organizations with tremendous social programs, but they simply deny the power of God. From the Holy Spirit inspiration, Paul wrote that our message and preaching are with a demonstration of the Spirit's power.

I am going to tell you what God feels when you know him, worship him, and praise him, but do not trust in him in the time of need for healing or deliverance. It may be scary. If it is, it is because of lack of knowledge and lack of faith.

In 2 Chronicles 15–16, there is a shocking story of a king who did a great job in the beginning of his reign, a great job in the sight of the Lord. He led the people of Judah back to God after a very long period of time of idol worship. He had the high places destroyed and reestablished the integral observance of the Lord's ordinances and commands.

King Asa trusted in the Lord, and he was accustomed to seek the counsel of the Most High for every decision, especially concerning warfare. He knew the Lord God Almighty had always granted his people victory whenever they sought him or cried out to him. In Exodus 3:7–8, God spoke to Moses: "The Lord said, 'I have indeed seen the misery of my people in Egypt. I have heard them crying out because of their slave drivers, and I am concerned about their suffering. So I have come down to rescue them.'"

King Asa reorganized his government together with the functions of the priests and teachers of the law in accordance with the prescriptions that God gave Moses. He showed such integrity in obeying God's voice and respecting and honoring God's messengers or prophets that he ordered that, whoever did not worship the Lord God of Israel and obey his commands, would be put to death. He deposited his grandmother Maacah from her position as queen mother because she had made a repulsive Asherah pole, a pagan idol the Israelites were worshiping. In 2 Chronicles 15:16, the king had the pole broken and burnt, but he did not utterly destroy or remove the high places where the idol worshiping had taken place.

When we are in Christ, we are a new creation. Everything we were in the world has gone. Whatever remains that we still do or practice will be an open door for the enemy or adversary to get hold of us, even defeat us. The Bible says in 1Peter 5:8: "Be self-controlled and alert. Your enemy the devil prowls around like a roaring lion looking for someone to devour." We must be extremely cautious about how to live our new life in Christ, avoiding at all cost to give glory to the devil by our actions and way of thinking. In 2 Chr 15:17, the sliding point of King Asa's downfall occurs. "Although he did not remove the high places from Israel, Asa's heart was fully committed to the Lord all his life." Second Chronicles 15:19 says: "There was no more war until the thirty-fifth year of Asa's reign." God had granted him peace because of his integrity.

The consequences of not totally abiding in the will of the Lord began in the thirty-sixth year of his rein, in 2 Chr 16.

Through their own brothers, Israel, the enemy, came up to attack Judah. Now Asa forgot about the Lord his God. He refused to seek the counsel from the prophets of God. Rather, he sought rescue from a pagan nation. "Where is your faith?" says the Lord. Faith without works is dead by itself. And the works of faith is obedience to the Lord's commands and practice of the word of God in its full integrity.

Abraham believed God by performing his instructions, and the Bible says this was counted to him as righteousness. We were not able before. Because God is able, the Savior Yeshua came and died for us to make us able. That is why it is written: Philippians 4:13, "I can do all things through Christ who strengthens me"(NKJV). Your downfall begins at the place where you start putting your trust in men or world instead of the Lord God Almighty. Downfall from your walk with God is when you, believer of Christ, trust more in medical science than in the same Christ as healer. The Bible is clear about this. The Word of God is the truth.

The end of Asa is really sad. Second Chronicles 16:7–10 states: "At that time Hanani the seer came to Asa king of Judah and said to him: "Because you rely on the king of Aram and not on the Lord your God, the army of the king of Aram has escaped from your hand. Were not the Cushites and Libyans a mighty army with great numbers of chariots and horsemen? Yet when you relied on the Lord, He delivered them into your hand. For the eyes of the Lord range throughout the earth to strengthen those whose hearts are fully committed to him. You have done a foolish thing, and from now on, you will be at war." Asa was angry with the seer because of this; He was so enraged that he put him in prison. At the same time, Asa brutally oppressed some of the people. I urge you to read 2 Chr:12–13 with more attention and meditation. "In the thirty-ninth year of his reign Asa was afflicted with a disease in his feet. Though his disease was severe, even in his illness, he did not seek help from the Lord, but only from the physicians. Then in his forty-first year of reign Asa died."

Children of God, it is very important to train yourselves not to lean onto your own understanding, but to acknowledge the Lord in all your ways. Have faith in God and power of his might so he will uphold you with his righteous right hand, especially in time of need. Trust in him always. He will love to meet with you in your secret place of prayer to commune with you. Even right now, he is knocking at the door of your heart. He keeps telling you that he is the Lord who heals you. If your ears are not sharpened enough to hear him, read his Word. The Lord said he does not take pleasure when the sinner dies, but he does take much more pleasure when the sinner repents and turns from his or her wicked ways (paraphrased from the entire Ezekiel 18). "For God so loved the world that He gave His only begotten Son, that whoever believes in Him should not perish but have everlasting life." John 3:16 (NKJV) That is you and I. He sent his precious son to fulfill our healing, deliverance, peace and joy, happiness, and victory on the cross at Golgotha. The mysterious works of salvation done at the cross at Golgotha was the final solution to the problem of health in human society.

We have been living these past two thousand years in an extraordinary dispensation, but, unfortunately, the closer we get to the end, the more we take the veracity of God's spiritual power for granted in the churches. It is time for all of us to shake off the dust and wake up. Yes, a wake-up call is now sounding stronger and stronger.

I want to pray with you.

Abba Father, I thank you for who you are and for your great love and mercy for your children. I thank you so much for the divine revelation of your healing and deliverance power. Just as you snatched us from the hand of the enemy and took us out of darkness into your marvelous light, you also made us whole by the blood of the Lamb. Yes, Father, you want us to prosper not only spiritually and materially, but also and much more physically. This is because you know everything. You know, Father, that, without health, we are just nothing but burden. Without you, we can do nothing. I thank you for who you are because you are the Lord our healer, hence because we are now healed by the stripes and through the blood of Yeshua in the name that is above all names, Yeshua Hamashiach, the Son of the Living God. Thank you, Lord. Amen.

Mark 11:24 says, "Therefore I tell you, whatever you ask in prayer, believe that you have received it, and it will be yours." Do you believe? Say, "Yes, thank you, Yeshua. All the glory is to the Lord."

What a wonderful name we have received! Yeshua! There is no other name I know but Yeshua. What a wonderful gift from God. The Ruach Kodesh (Holy Spirit) is the giver of these gifts. First Corinthians 12 gives us full details of the gifts of the Holy Spirit in the church. Through his vessel, Paul, he teaches us how they operate. If you keep trusting in God and seek him alone with all your heart, you will certainly avoid all the troubles or side effects that medications may occasion into your life. Many are tired of long years of physical weakness and failure, with unceasing absorption of tons of medication. This is the Word of he who is faithful and true.

"Come to me, all you who labor and are heavy laden, and I will give you rest. Take my yoke upon you and learn from me, for I am gentle and lowly in heart, and you will find rest for your souls. For My yoke is easy and my burden is light" (Matt 11:28–30 NKJV).

Part II
Origin of Diseases and the Curses

The Different Categories of Mankind Curses

I am now going to present the origin of diseases. The suffering and tribulation of man on Earth today can be analyzed in different ways and at different levels: individual, family, community, national, and worldwide. The beginning of any human health problem has its foundation in words of curses spoken by God as verdict because he is a righteous judge.

When I develop the results of the spiritual diagnosis of the world sicknesses, I neither intend to discourage those who are suffering physically or mentally nor try to express a judgment on sick people. One more time, my message is that of hope to those who do not know Christ personally as the healer of mankind. I am sharing the result of research and revelation to help you understand the causes of evil in order to grasp the key to the gate of salvation, healing, and deliverance. And, for those who know Christ personally and have experienced his grace and mercy at any level, let this analysis be a work tool for teaching prayer and intercession.

Now, I will also present the different kinds of pain generated by the presence of unclean spirits that are surrounding our society.

I have heard and dealt with many questions similar to these. Why do people suffer so much in this world? Life is full of pain, fight and hurt, disease, and premature death. We live in a time when we are experiencing more pains, troubles, and devastating diseases. The answer goes as far back as the disconnection of man's relationship with the Holy God, his creator. I considered the word of God and summarized the answer with one word, disobedience. There are curses in the world, and we can either avoid or embrace them. On the contrary, blessings are around us. We can either embrace them or walk away from them.

The entire human race is suffering from curses that are the consequences of disobedience, disrespect, and rebellion. Deuteronomy 28 clearly shows that God's blessing to man will manifest in his life as a result of his obedience to God's command.

This is in the first fourteen verses. The second part of this chapter has always shaken my brain. The day I took time to meditate on this particular passage and found out that even headaches and fever, which are always taken for granted, are manifestations of curses or consequences of some disobedience somewhere in our lives, I said to myself, "This is serious." We are in a very serious business dealing with God's matters. Is it not written about him that "…Holy, Holy, Holy is the Lord God Almighty…"? Revelation 4:8. He is seated on the throne of holiness, and everything around him must be holy. God expects us to be holy in every area of our life because he made us in his holy image. Holiness implies healthy soul and spirit within a healthy body.

The Word of God reveals three categories of curses that mankind has been suffering from: Curses pronounced directly by God's face to man's sin; Curses pronounced by fathers against their children; Curses that anyone could draw to himself as a result of neglecting some divine principles.

The more we become aware of this, the higher we climb the ladder of victory that will lead us to the place where we can really say we are seated with Christ in the heavenly place, in accordance with Eph 2:4–6, "But because of His great love for us, God, who is rich in mercy, made us alive with Christ even when we were dead in transgressions—it is by grace you have been saved. And God raised us up with Christ and seated us with Him in the heavenly realms in Christ Jesus."

Glory to God our Father, and thank him, for, in Christ Jesus, we are far above the curses, if and only if we know how to walk with him.

The Divine Maledictions: Curses Pronounced by God

The curses pronounced directly from the mouth of God to man were not the expressions of impotent wishes, but they carry their effects with them and are attended with all the miseries they denounce or foretell. We should not take those curses for granted, bearing in mind that they are expressions of useless wishes. They are carried out with total accuracy. Let us see how our good God has made us so marvelously and gave us dominion over the rest of the creatures and how, unfortunately, man has been at the origin of his own troubles and downfall on Earth.

In the beginning, God created all things visible and invisible.

Then He said, Genesis 1:26-27, "Let us make man in our image, in our likeness, and let them rule over the fish of the sea and the birds of the air, over the livestock, over all the earth, and over all the creatures that move along the ground.." So God made man and gave him the power over every creation existing on

Earth. Know that, in this original state, there was no knowledge of disobedience, rebellion, evil, or their consequences. In this first state of human existence, there was no knowledge of cancer, diabetes, heart attacks, headaches, fever, and so forth. God even specified that man should rule over the serpent, the devil. The last part of the above verse is very interesting. When God is giving dominion to man over every living thing, he is showing the presence of the devil around this man, and he is telling him that he has the power to overcome the devil. "The creatures that move along the ground" means the reptile that crawls. Revelation 12:9 says, "So the great dragon was cast out, that serpent of old, called the devil and satan, who deceives the whole world;..." (NKJV). It is obvious that, when Eve was drawn into the serpent's snare to the tree of the knowledge of good and evil, she was dealing directly with satan. Satan was there when God was creating all things. He heard God speak to man with love and kindness, affection, and friendship, and he was jealous. I will expound on satan so the reader will have knowledge of man's number one enemy, his governmental organization, his schemes, and strategies launched toward your downfall and destruction.

When God had completed his creative work, he had not put any pain or disease in Adam's body. As I said earlier, there was no knowledge of pain in Adam's vocabulary. His communion with the Lord was as such as he was dwelling in the shelter of the Most High. He was resting in the shadow of the Almighty. God's protection was his shield and rampart. Adam could not do anything without consulting his Heavenly Father. In fact, there was no other man beside him who was above his authority. God was the authority over Adam, and they both had good communication.

The way God made man in comparison with the way he created all other living beings deserves to draw our full attention. Remember that God is very explicit in his manner of expression. The Word made all things. "And God said, "Let there be light..." Gen 1:3. And, from nowhere and nothing, a huge source of solar energy was suspended in the cosmic space, displaying powerful light all around the firmament. From this time on, it is very important to notice the presence Ruach Kodesh when God is getting ready to display his splendor. Just before God spoke the Word, his spirit was hovering over the waters. Ruach Kodesh, the generator of God's glorious manifestation, was there to operate the creative power through the Word. God spoke the Word, and things appeared from nonexistence into existence.

Hebrews 11:3 says, "By faith we understand that the universe was formed at God's command, so that what is seen was not made out of what was visible." But God did not say, "Let there be man," did he?

The making and shaping of man was a very serious affair to undertake. The divine throne was (and still is) surrounded by living beings and great multitudes of angels serving and worshipping God day and night. The Son of God, the one known as the firstborn among the brethren, was right by the side of the Father in all his glory. The Holy Spirit was there, getting ready to dwell in the upcoming human temple. In 1Cor 3:16 it says, "Do you not know that you are the temple of God and that the Spirit of God dwells in you?" we are the temple of God because the Spirit of God lives in us. But this is only true when the Holy Spirit dwells in us and operates the divine transformation of our mind and restoration of our body. Someone can be the temple of demons, not of God. Just because people have heard preachers say we are the temple of God or have read this verse from the Scriptures and because of their lack of teaching or knowledge, they think they are the temple of God. You are not always what you think you are or what you are told you are. This was effectively true at creation, but, today, a certain number of criteria have to be met in order to consider oneself a temple of the Living God.

I have come across men whose lives were totally messed up with alcohol, sexual immorality, and other things of that sort and who had never experienced the true salvation in Christ Jesus. They said to my face, "I am God's temple." I have heard this several times, even from unbelievers who did not recognize the Lord Jesus Christ. I understand their bodies are also temples, but unclean spirits, not God, have made their home there. The wonderful part here is that our Lord gave us the assignment to cast out those unclean spirits and set the captives free so they can really become temples of the Holy Spirit.

The entire creation was anxious to witness the coming into existence of a man image of the Creator himself. Consider that an extraordinary interplanetary conference was held. During which, an important decision was going to be executed when God spoke and said, "Let us make man in our image..." Then he emphasized, "...in our likeness..." Gen. 1:26.

The making and shaping of man took place after God had completed the creation of the heavens and earth and all things therein, including the trees that bear fruit to eat, the beast of the field, the birds, and the fish. God had already put together every blessing to make man happy.

In what sense did God make man in his image? God is not flesh, but spirit. In Gen 2:7, it says, "The Lord God formed the man from the dust of the ground and breathed into his nostrils the breath of life, and the man became a living soul." Adam became a living soul by the breath of God and received dominion or power over the creatures. Similarly, in John 20:22, Jesus breathes the Holy Spirit to empower the disciples. "And with that He breathed on them and said: 'Receive the Holy Spirit.'"

Man was made in the image of God by the breath of life that is the Spirit. And God loved him. He loved him so much that he did not want to see him live alone among the beasts. Then he made them male and female and blessed them tremendously. He gave them everything they needed to make them happy. He gave them the power and authority over every creature. Adam and Eve had intimate communication with the Father.

The relationship between man and the Creator was so beautiful that God took a lot of pleasure in coming down occasionally to walk and talk with him. They used to have serious conversation about different topics. God would sometimes draw the animals to Adam so he would give them a name. God also placed man in a beautiful garden to cultivate. He made Adam the owner of all the riches of the ground. He gave Adam the opportunity to enjoy all the natural and supernatural resources that were at his disposal in his environment. Genesis 2:12 says, "And the gold of that land is good: there is bdellium and the onyx stone." Genesis 2:15 says, "And the Lord God took the man, and put him into the garden of Eden to work it and take care of it."

Because sin had not overtaken man at this time, Adam was holy, free from sin, and in perfect communion with God. He was the pinnacle of God's creation and given the authority to govern Earth and subdue it. He was given the responsibility and accountability of working under the direction of God in caring for his creation.

Adam and Eve were very happy as they enjoyed the glorious presence of the Creator, together with his love and protection. They had no knowledge of sin and its consequences because they were created holy.

In order to understand our level of power and glory in Christ, we must look at how wonderfully we were made and how important we are to God. He is our Heavenly Father, and we are his sons and daughters.

"In the beginning was the Word, and the Word was with God, and the Word was God. The same was in the beginning with God. All things were made by Him; and without Him was not anything made that was made. In Him was life; and the life was the light of men (John 1:1–4)."

The beginning of both Genesis and John presents the existence of all things made possible by the word of God, his law. In the Lord was life for eternity, and the life was the light of men. In their state of holiness and purity, Adam and Eve, together with their children, were to live forever because they had no knowledge of sin and its consequences. Eden and human life were comparable to that of the paradise of God. As God wanted to test man's faith and obedience, he placed the tree of life in the midst of the garden, along with the tree of the knowledge of good and evil. The presence of the tree of life was the evidence of life eternal that God gave man in his state of holiness and purity, as it is specified in Rev 2:7. "To him that overcomes will I give to eat of the tree of life, which is in the midst of the paradise of God." God created humans as moral beings with the ability to choose freely to love and obey the Creator or to disobey him and rebel against his will. The first law of prohibition was given to man when God placed the tree of the knowledge of good and evil before man and told him not to eat of it.

Right from this moment, the word of God revealed his law. Why should he, being omniscient and all-knowing, then pour out the conditional evidence of life? He certainly knew Earth would turn to flesh and sin was already lying there in wait for its revelation. And sin is revealed through the prohibition, "...you shall not ..." of Gen 2:16, NKJV. But, in all these, the coming of Christ was predestined before even God said, "Let there be light..." (Gen 1:3). In other words, we were predestined to be partakers of his glorious kingdom in Christ before the foundation of the world. Eph 1:3–4 says, "Blessed be the God and Father of our Lord Jesus Christ, who has blessed us with every spiritual blessing in the heavenly places in Christ, just as He chose us in Him before the foundation of the world, that we should be holy and without blame before Him in love, having predestined us to adoption as sons by Jesus Christ to Himself, according to the good pleasure of His will." (NKJV). The coming of Jesus Christ the Savior was planned before Adam was made. Oh, what a depth of the non-understandable divine science and hidden knowledge of God! He is worthy to be glorified at all times.

It is very important to meditate on Gen 2:16–17, as to how God instructs with direct result or consequence following obedience or disobedience. "And the Lord God commanded the man, saying, 'You are free to eat from any tree in the garden; but you must not eat from the tree of the knowledge of good and evil, for when you eat of it you will surely die.'"

The end of this passage clearly shows us again that man would have lived eternally if he had not transgressed the law of God. Disobedience will bring death, but, before death, it will bring everything that causes death, including disease, illness, sorrow, and different calamities.

Since the creation, mankind has been bound to God through belief in and obedience to his word as divine principle and absolute truth. Life eternal through faith and obedience to the Lord's commands is demonstrated all throughout the Scriptures as the governing principle in Adam's relationship to God in the Garden of Eden. Adam was warned that he would die if he transgressed the Law of God by eating of the forbidden tree. The same principle continues to govern our lives today. Death is the direct consequence of rebellion against the divine order. In John 9, Jesus said, "Whosoever believes in me shall not see death." In effect, believing in Jesus was (and still is) the prerequisite of salvation and therefore of restoration to the holy and righteous man. God made this very strong statement to warn Adam, "For the day you will eat (or disobey me), you will surely die." Genesis 2:17

When we look at churches today, we can still verify that man has walked away from God's command. The power of the gospel has been rejected because of immorality and incredibility. But the gospel came to mankind as the accomplishment of the divine plan of salvation from death and every element that has caused death since the sad event of the garden of Eden. The gospel is the good news of the kingdom of God. In other words, the Church is supposed to be the place of the restoration of every human being who has manifested faith and obedience to God. The restoration, in general, comes through the blood of the Lamb that was slain at the place of man, the Lamb of God who removes our sin.

The word of God is warning mankind with even stronger commands in the New Testament. In Christ, we are the light of the world, so our light must shine. The Bible clearly says in 2Cor. 5:17, "Therefore, if anyone is in Christ, he is a new creation; the old has gone, the new has come!" It is true that the old Adamic nature must be gone. The result of salvation through the Messiah is first the restoration of health, strength, and power, which is physical salvation generating peace with God and joy within our soul.

But it is not everyone who claims to be saved that enjoys the physical salvation or health, as the Lord himself said in Matt 7:21, "Not everyone who says to me, 'Lord, Lord' will enter the Kingdom of heaven, but only he who does the will of my Father who is in heaven." Clearly, not everyone who has church membership, claims to be child of God, goes to church every Sunday, gives a lot of money to build the temple, or sings beautiful songs to praise the Lord will experience the fullness of life in Christ and his spiritual and physical blessings. Only he who obeys the commands of the Lord and puts his divine principle into practice in all its integrity can fully enjoy the power of health. In Rom 6:23, it says, "The wages of sin is death." Ezekiel 18:4 says, "The soul who sins is the one who will die." The consequence of disobedience that was pronounced by God to Adam is still the same today. The Word of God (Yeshua Hamashiach) is the same yesterday, today, and forever.

Cursed Is the Ground

Since man was made with the ground, if cursed is the ground, then cursed is the man. We think that, if we were at Adam's place, we would have repented right there and gotten the situation fixed. It is not true. From the moment one command was transgressed, the entire law of the creation was transgressed as well. Pride, jealousy, hatred, fear, oppression, and so forth entered the heart of man. See what Cain did to his brother Abel.

Adam and Eve lost their wonderful communion they had with the Lord after they disobeyed God's command. They were not to eat from the tree of the knowledge of good and bad. And, because they had disobeyed, they had to bear the consequences.

This is why Adam and Eve ran away from God and hid themselves. Because of his love and fatherly compassion, God came to them.

> If Adam had fallen on his knees, repented right away, and asked God for forgiveness, I believe the verdicts

pronounced would not have been as severe as they were. But, instead, Adam tried to impute his sin to God by seeking a good reason why he disobeyed, giving an excuse for disobedience that would make any person more upset. This is the word of God. Genesis 3:6–12 says, "When the woman saw that the fruit of tree was good for food and pleasing to the eye, and also desirable for gaining wisdom, she took some and ate it. She also gave some to her husband, who was with her, and he ate it. Then the eyes of both of them were opened, and they realized they were naked; so they saw fig leaves together and made coverings for themselves. Then the man and his wife heard the sound of the Lord God as He was walking in the garden in the cool of the day, and they hid from the Lord God among the trees of the garden. But the Lord God called to the man, "Where are you?" He answered: "I heard you in the garden, and I was afraid because I was naked, so I hid." And He said: "Who told you that you were naked? Have you eaten from the tree that I commanded you not to eat from?"

At this particularly crucial time, a child of God must repent right away and ask the Lord for forgiveness. In the church today, Christians always have good reason to obey the voice of the devil, sin against God, and even despise the Lord. People lean to their own understanding and try to be wise to their own eyes. They pretend they acknowledge the Lord in their ways, but they lie and use God's word, which they distort to their advantage in order to prove themselves right. They make their case worse and their sentence more terrible. Death, heart attack, cancer, stroke, and more are at the forefront of our society's agenda. Listen to the man's answer to the Lord God. God said, "I commanded you not to eat from."

"The man said, "The woman you put here with me, she gave me some fruit from the tree, and I ate it." Gen. 3:12 This kind of answer would stir up any person's anger. How could God, who is so sensitive to sin, not be angry? I believe that, if Adam had just fallen on his knees, acknowledged his sin, repented, and cried for forgiveness, things would have been somehow different. God does not take pleasure when the sinner dies, but he takes much more pleasure when the sinner repents and turns from his wicked ways. Adam sinned and continued to sin by challenging God with excuses.

This is the cause of the downfall of man. Gen 3:17, "To Adam he said, "Because you listen to your wife and ate from the tree about which I commanded you, 'You must not eat of it,' cursed is the ground because of you. Through painful toil you will eat of it all the days of your life." Genesis 3:19 says, "By the sweat of your brow, you will eat your food until you return to the ground, since from it you were taken; for dust you are and to dust you will return.".

This is the first time God the Father, who is love, spoke words of curses to man. Let us pause at the end of Gen 3:17 and transfer the situation onto every human thereafter. Any time we, man or women, disobey God, we get the same results. Eve also disobeyed God. After that, they both used excuses. It will surely occur because the Word of God is the same today as it was then. "Through painful toil you will eat, and you will suffer until you die." The blood of Yeshua will not do anything for you just because you believe in him and are a church member who pays your tithes, sings with a beautiful voice in a great choir, or does a lot of social work. They are also very important, of course. But it takes more than that to fully enjoy your salvation.

The precious and priceless blood of Yeshua will have no effect in your life just because of your degrees in or knowledge of theology. You would be deceived, like many others, who have been led astray through false doctrines introduced by the deceiver since the early days of the New Testament Church. Acts 20:29–30 says "For I know this, that after my departure savage wolves will come in among you, not sparing the flock. Also from among yourselves men will rise up, speaking perverse things, to draw away the disciples after themselves."

> Paul was led by the Holy Spirit to foresee the downfall of the church people under satan's dominion, just like Eve and then Adam. The same warning is emphasized by Peter to the Body of Christ, in 2 Pet 3:16–17:[A] s also in all his epistles, speaking in them of these things, in which are some things hard to understand, which untaught and unstable people twist to their own destruction, as they do also the rest of the Scriptures. You therefore, beloved, since you know this beforehand, beware lest you also fall from your own steadfastness, being led away with the error of the wicked.

It is extremely dangerous to listen to men and practice the tradition of men instead of listening to the voice of the Lord and obeying his command. Adam had free will, but he used Eve as an excuse.

Genesis 3:23 speaks of the banishment from Eden. "The Lord

God banished him from the Garden of Eden to work the ground from which he had been taken."

> And the word of the Prophet Isaiah comes true in their lives: But your iniquities have separated you from your God; your sins have hidden His face from you, so that He will not hear. For your hands are stained with blood, and your fingers with guilt. Your lips have spoken lies, and your tongue mutters wicked things (Isa 59:2–3).

Even now we hear that abortions (committed or promoted), hatred, and murder are all found in the church. Just as through the Prophet Isaiah, God is speaking to Israel, his people. He never stopped sending warnings, instructions, and guidance to his church, demonstrating his love and compassion, along with his mercy and faithfulness. In spite of the curses, the world is going through, "God so loved the world that He gave His only begotten Son (Jesus Christ) that whosoever believes in Him should not perish, but have everlasting life." John 3:16, (NKJV). To him be all the glory and honor and power forever and ever. Amen.

Every other curse and its cause originates from the original sin of disobedience, as we have just studied. We normally become slaves to sin by obeying the voice of the sinful nature. However, we will not neglect to mention other declarations of curses made by the Almighty God in a state of disappointment and anger.

You Are Under a Curse

The second time God ever spoke words of curses was against Cain, who killed his brother Abel. The sinful nature of man was no more hidden just in the flesh or in the heart, but the actions preceding the heart's desire were now implemented to their full extent. Out of jealousy and wickedness, which combined together to use the anger spirit, Cain committed the first crime in the history of mankind. The Scriptures advise us not to let the sun go down on our anger. It is not the anger itself that is dreadful, but it is every action or decision following that state of mind that is dangerous and the sentences thereof. The painful, even distressful, problem of murder is not new. The consequences of taking someone's life or shedding innocent blood are terrible and frightening.

This sentence is one of the harshest declarations God pronounced because of sin. Genesis 4:10–11 says, "The Lord said, 'What have you done? Listen! Your brother's blood cries out to me from the ground. Now you are under a curse and driven from the ground, which opened its mouth to receive your brother's blood from your hand.'"

Now Cain's murder has made things worse. The sentence is once more curse to the ground. Genesis 4:12 says, "When you work the ground, it will no longer yield its crops for you. You will be a restless wanderer on the earth." The characteristics of the sinful nature grew more with their accompanying consequences until the Lord decided to get rid of sin by destroying the living beings with water. After the banishment from Eden, it did not take too long for man to begin to experience bitterness, the full extent of hatred, and even murder.

Understand that God does not want us to perish or be cursed. He has made us in his image. He has granted us the extraordinary capability of consciousness of good and evil and the knowledge of life and death. He has given us the power of choice so we cannot put the blame on anybody else when we do wrong or go astray.

When Prophet Nathan made King David aware of his sin, he fell before the Lord, face to the ground, and repented bitterly. Although he was known as the man according to God's own heart, he suffered the consequences of adultery and crime all his life. Colossians 3:25 says, "Anyone who does wrong will be repaid for his wrong, and there is no favoritism."

Exodus 15:26 is a very powerful verse that many people quote (and we hope that it works). But most of the time, the quote is not complete. We always hear only the very last part of it. "I am the Lord, who heals thee." This is true. It is also (and more importantly) true that the healing takes place more effectively if and only if we fulfill our part. That is God's way of doing business, and there is no other way around it. To be happy in the Lord, there is no other way but to trust in him and obey his commands. In full, Exodus 15:26 says, "He said: 'If you listen carefully to the voice of the Lord your God and do what is right is His eyes, if you pay attention to His commands and keep all his decrees, I will not bring on you any of the diseases I brought on the Egyptians, for I am the Lord, who heals you.'" Exodus 15:25 is important to make note of. "There the Lord made a decree and a law for them, and there He tested them." This passage is fully analyzed later.

The promises of God for healing or blessings given in a timely and accurate manner are dually declared with conditions. Some people call this a win-win business that is impossible for man to handle. It is obvious that we undergo some of the tests or trials on the part of our Heavenly Father. These tests come for us to prove our trust in the Lord, our confidence in the Word, and promises of God and be made stronger in our walk with God because we are still in a spiritual battlefield.

Unfortunately, we often fail the test, like those children of Israel in the wilderness, because we focus more on our circumstances and consider our physical environment more than the things from on high. Even though we know Jesus said in Matthew 6:33, "But seek first his kingdom and his righteousness, and all these things will be given to you as well," we place so much confidence on what we see. We have faith when we substantially live in what we do not see. How can you say you have faith in what you see? Faith is seeing with your spiritual eyes what your natural eyes do not see. The Bible says, Hebrews 11:6, "And without faith, it is impossible to please God."

Salvation from the Flood

When God dealt with Noah to save himself and his family from the terrible flood, the Lord had poured his anointing and power upon the man because he had found Noah righteous in his sight. We also understand that God never forsook the righteous in the time of massive destruction. The work Noah did in building such a majestic and gigantic masterpiece was not done with the natural human strength or wisdom, especially at that time.

Today, we may admire the wonders of science and technology when we see the wonderful realizations of all times, starting from huge ships and submarines to jumbo aircrafts and spaceships. The gradual technical and industrial revolutions in the past two to three centuries are putting us in a place where we can accept or understand the logic of the mathematics and physical science behind these realizations.

But I want to show here that, about five thousand years ago, the construction of such a mysterious and huge ship evident or thinkable. In order for a man to act and do things that are beyond human capacity of thinking, he must be led by a supernatural power, in this case, the power of God. In fact, because God found Noah righteous, the man had to be highly anointed with the Spirit of God in order to commune with the Most High at that level where God could be giving him accurate instructions that he executed with perfect accuracy. There is a way to believe that God himself was building the ark; Noah was just being a vessel. His walk, talk, and thought were so fully those of God that he could not make (or was not even allowed) a mistake in the implementation of God's plan. Noah's walk and works with the Lord is an example that the New Testament believers ought to consider very closely because the least mistake on the part of this man would have generated tremendous damages over two hundred days of flood. Any eventual wreck would have terminated the existence of mankind and beasts on Earth.

Many church people today have lost their focus on Christ, like Peter who was walking on the water. He heard the sound of a wind blow and ceased to focus on the Word of God that was flesh right in front of him, on the surface of the great lake. He began to sink as soon as he turned his attention to the wind. So turning away from Christ will cause them to sink as individuals, as well as families and even entire congregations, cities, or nations. These mistakes occur every day and frequently take our eyes off the light of truth, faith, and courage. We begin to focus on things and suggestions of the flesh. That is why we sink in different manners. And when we sink, we find trouble in the depth of the waters. We find sorrows and more on a dry land was not

In the days of Noah, Earth was full of evil. Satan had subdued mankind at such a point that every thought and actions were wicked. The Bible says the Lord was grieved because of man's increasing wickedness. The Lord even:

Repented to have made man on the earth, and it grieved him at His heart. And the Lord said: "I will destroy man whom I have created from the face of the earth," Gen 6:6–7.

Stop this journey only a minute, and think of God repenting to have made man. This should make you shiver from your head to your toes. But I thank the Lord with all my heart for his great compassion for He loved the world so much that He kept preparing for the works of Golgotha. He had preserved a righteous man, to be the remnant.

In order for God to plan the complete eradication of human life from Earth, he must have surely been seriously hurt. He certainly had great pain on his heart. He was seated on his throne of glory watching over Earth and regularly seeing the extreme abomination, murder, perversion, and wickedness at such a level that no one could describe. As he was meditating on all these, he was also remembering the wonderful time spent in the garden of Eden with the pure and holy-hearted Adam. But, at the same time that his hurt was turning to anger, his love and compassion stirred up his mercy. He came down to work salvation through a righteous man, Noah, a type of Jesus in the sense of preserving or saving. First Thessalonians 1:10 says, "And to wait for his Son from heaven, whom he raised from the dead—Jesus who rescues us from the coming wrath." Second Peter 3:10–14 says: But the day of the Lord will come like a thief.

The heavens will disappear with a roar; the elements will be destroyed by fire, and the earth and everything in it will be laid bare. Since everything will be destroyed in this way, what kind of people ought you to be? You ought to live holy and godly lives as you look forward to the day of God and speed its coming. That day will bring about the destruction of the heavens by fire, and the elements will melt in the heat. But in keeping with his promise we are looking forward to a new heaven and a new earth, the home of righteousness. So then, dear friends, since you are looking forward to this, make every effort to be found spotless, blameless, and at peace with him.

We need to be aware that ungodliness provokes God to wrath. When sin and all abominations involved has reach a climax level, God's wrath will bring about destruction. But I continuously thank the Lord for his mercy and unfailing love because he has and will always preserve a remnant of righteous people for him.

These passages warn explicitly and get God's people to prepare for the day of the Lord. We are living in a crucial time of turmoil when biblical signs and foretold events are occurring to our hearing. In this precise time, God is watching over the Noah of today, the righteous ones who are righteous by their deeds and obedience to God's command to build the ark. Our ark today is that of salvation and holiness. Our ark today is in Christ Jesus. If anyone is in Christ, he is in an ark/ship of new creativity in a spiritual and physical healing and restoration clinic. Society today has been so brainwashed that we cannot be holy, even in Christ, because the flesh is weak. Lying tongues have succeeded in engraving that ideology in people's belief. It is a sad thing. Many passages in the Bible talk about holy men of God. First Peter 1:15 says, "But just as He who called you is holy, so be holy in all you do."

The Scriptures qualifies some great biblical figures as holy men (or women) of God. They feared the Lord, hated sin, and shunned evil, just as God described his servant Job before the biggest trials of all times that a man could encounter.

Noah was a holy man of God, righteous in all his ways. Genesis 6:9 says, "This is the account of Noah. Noah was a righteous man, blameless among the people of his time, and he walked with God." For this reason, God could save him and his family from the flood, manifesting his love and compassion and, most importantly, working out his continuous plan of Golgotha salvation. For God so loved the world that he used one righteous man to save mankind. This was a phase within the process of the divine plan for you and me today.

It is important to know that we cannot walk and commune with God unless we are found righteous and blameless in his sight. In the highly corrupted city of Sodom and Gomorrah that God was going to destroy, he spared Lot, whom he found righteous among the people of that city. God obviously still has some righteous men in the corrupted society of today's world, who are true disciples of the Lord Jesus Christ and love to put the word of God in practice in its full integrity. These disciples must have such great faith in the divine healing power as we can see it operated in the early church, the church of the Acts of the Apostles.

God said to Ezekiel that he was seeking just one who would stand in the gap for the nation so he would bring healing and deliverance. But, unfortunately, he could find no one. God needs you to stand in the gap. Ezekiel 22:30, "I looked for a man among them who would build up a wall and stand before me in the Gap on behalf of the land so I would not have to destroy it, but I found none." God wants to work with a remnant of faithful believers who will depend only on him and have confidence only in him because God has never (and will never share) his glory with anyone or fail anyone.

Noah stood in the gap for the entire humanity as he obeyed and followed God's instruction and built the ark to its perfect completion. He sheltered his family and all the living creatures in accordance with the Lord's accurate instructions.

The Curse of Noah

Noah had three sons: Shem, Ham, and Japheth. They all did a mighty job with their father in building the ark. Noah and his family followed the Lord's words and certainly worked together as a team. When the construction was over, Gen 6:22 says, "Noah did everything just as God commanded him."

Genesis 7:1 says, "The Lord then said to Noah: 'Go into the ark, you and your whole family, because I have found you righteous in this generation.'"

And the flood came and wiped off every living thing on Earth except the occupants of Noah's ark.

After the flood, the human population on Earth was reduced to eight people. Noah, his wife, their three sons, and their sons' wives populated the world under a new covenant and blessing from the Lord their God. I urged the reader to go over Gen 9 and meditate on each verse. There should be an incredible profound thought over the deeds of the Almighty God. Genesis 9:1 says,

"God blessed Noah and his sons, saying to them, 'Be fruitful and increase in number and fill the earth.'"

When we look at the spiritual quality and mental capability of this eight-member family, we are moved to believe that they were going to multiply as a beginning generation of righteous people on a new Earth. We may think that, because God had just erased the wicked and abominable people from the face of the earth, this new human race would be a righteous one. It could have so, provided Noah did not bring a curse that satan, who was always around, began to manage well to his advantage to this day.

After the flood, life on Earth was renewed. Everything began afresh. The vegetable and animal world and mankind were all restored to purity. However, it remains obvious that the original curses pronounced by God in the Garden of Eden were still in force.

> The Bible tells clearly how Noah's curse entered the world. Genesis 9:18–24 says: The sons of Noah who came out of the ark were Shem, Ham and Japheth. These were the three sons of Noah and from them came the people who were scattered over the earth. Noah, a man of the soil, proceeded to plant a vineyard. When he drank some of its wine, he became drunk and lay uncovered inside his tent. Ham the father of Canaan, saw his father's nakedness and told his two brothers outside. But Shem and Japheth took a garment and laid it across their shoulders; then they walked in backward and covered their father's nakedness. Their faces were turned the other way so that they would not see their father's nakedness.

When Noah awoke from his wine and found out what his youngest son had done to him, he said,

"Cursed be Canaan! The lowest of slaves will he be to his brothers."

As mankind began to multiply and spread over Earth, the three sons departed each one to his remote territory, taking their progenitors and belongings with them. They left the place where the ark had landed at the end of the flood, the surrounding of Mount Ararat. The blessings God poured on them in Gen 9:1 was now reduced to two-thirds because one of them carried the father's curse along with him and his descendants forever. Noah received the blessings for everybody, but he cursed Ham's upcoming nations. He did not call Ham's name directly on the curse, except his son Canaan. Canaan will later be the territory of the Hebrews' conquest and occupation.

I have closely considered the different migrations of the descendants of Shem, Ham, and Japheth. The Bible states the descendants of Japheth went north and settled around the coastal regions of the Black Sea and north of (now) the Mediterranean Sea. They became progenitors of the Medes and Greeks, as well as the Caucasian races of Europe and part of Asia. Genesis 10:5 says, "From these the maritime people spread out into their territory by their clans within their nations, each with its own language."

Shem took the eastern direction and settled in Arabia and the Middle East Valley, toward Ur of Chaldeans. Abraham came out of Shem nation.

Ham and his children moved south. Canaan settled in the territory that bore his name. He was the father of Sidon of the Hittites, Jebusites, Amorites, Girgashites, Hivites, and so forth.

They were all the Canaanites, who the Israelites either destroyed or enslaved in later years. The other of Ham's children, Mizraim and Put, spread from Egypt over North Africa. Cush, the father of Nimrod (the great hunter of souls), settled in the area known later as Ethiopia. This is how the children of the cursed son of Noah spread in the continent of Africa and multiplied to become the black race.

Whereas the wisdom and intelligence of Japheth and Shem earned them tremendous blessing because of the way they showed respect to their father, the silliness of Ham caused his long-lasting misfortune.

> The curse of Noah upon Ham and his seed was clear and precise. Genesis 9:25–27 says: He said: "Cursed be Canaan! The lowest of slaves will he be to his brothers." He also said, "Blessed be the Lord, the God of Shem! (Prophesying God of Abraham, Isaac and Jacob.) May Canaan be the slave of Shem. May God extend the territory of Japheth; May Japheth live in the tents of Shem, and may Canaan be his slave."

The most terrible acts of slavery in the history of mankind remain that by Japheth's children over the black race. Even those who were not carried across the Atlantic Ocean suffered the bitterness of colonialism for many decades. Presently, they are being destroyed through the oppression of neocolonialism that is no other than the management of so-called economic independences and generation of civil and tribal fights all over the continent. Even to this day, many types of slavery are in the world. Yeshua said; "I tell you the truth, everyone who sins is a slave to sin." We were slaves of satan in our way of life and practice of bad deeds in God's eyes. But thanks and glory to God for Jesus Christ, his son. Whomever the son frees is free indeed. In Christ, we are free from Noah's curse because we are a new creation. The old has gone, and the blood of the Lamb of God has completely wiped it off.

Now you understand that generational curses or blessing can be carried over centuries and millennia. In Christ Jesus, we have been set free from every type of slavery, whether we came from Shem, Ham, or Japheth. The curse of the garden of Eden and that of Cain remain fully in force to this day in the flesh of all men. Jesus Christ set the whole mankind free from any bondage two thousand years ago on the cross at Golgotha. That is why he said, "For God so loved the world that He gave His only begotten Son, that whosoever believeth in Him should not perish, but have everlasting life" (John 3:16 KJV). Again, the awesome blessing of freedom from bondage that Jesus gives is free. That is God's grace, but it is taken by faith.

I want to draw the attention of parents who take pleasure to stay naked before their children, thinking it is normal and having no clue they are calling and transferring demonic spirits of slavery upon those children. The intensity of the curse of Noah and its impact on so many generations is proof that seeing parents' or anybody's nakedness is abomination in the eyes of God. This should not be taken for granted. I also advise parents, especially fathers, not to curse or even insult their children. It is damnation to your own blood for generations. Always bless them at all times.

Slavery is manifest in different areas of life. Some are slaves to extreme poverty, alcoholism, drugs, womanizing, or prostitution. Others are slaves to specific diseases, like generational curses of diabetes, cancer, ulcers, seizures, heart attacks, high blood pressure, and so forth.

When our Lord and Savior Jesus Christ gave up his spirit on the cross, he said these last words in John 19:30, "It is finished." So he proclaimed the fulfillment of our total freedom, the implementation of the salvation plan, as stated in Gen 3:15, "He will crush your head; Therefore, there is no concrete reason to be in Christ and remain slave of this present age at the same time."

The Curses of the Law

Since the first curse in the garden of Eden occurred because of disobedience, it was fully established that anyone who does not obey God's command would experience some consequences, no matter how heavy or light they may seem to be. Any sad or painful result for turning away from the grace and love of God is classified as curse.

Because curse has occurred from disobedience to God, it is, by itself, manifested through pains and sufferings of various types.

Moses' Ministry was especially characterized by the establishment of law for the children of Israel. But the law could not save them. Rather, it brought more curses to mankind. It was very hard for man to abide in God's life regulations and his command. When Jesus was on Earth and teaching his disciples, they became concerned at some time to the point of questioning. "Who then can be saved? But Jesus looked at them and said to them: 'With men, this is impossible, but with God, all things are possible'" (Matt 19:25–26 NKJV).

The curses stated in the Bible for specific wrongdoings and bad activities should be subjects of deep concerns for the believers. I will quote a few of them.

Deuteronomy 27:9–10 (NKJV) says, "Then Moses and the priests, the Levites, spoke to all Israel, saying: 'Take heed and listen, O Israel: This day you have become the people of the Lord your God. Therefore you shall obey the voice of the Lord your God, and observe His commandments and His statutes which I command you today.'"

Let us consider the following verses and begin to understand why there are so much evil and pains in the world.

> Deuteronomy 27:14–20 says: And the Levites shall speak with a loud voice and say to all the men of Israel: Cursed is the one who makes a carved or molded image, an abomination to the Lord, the work of the hands of the craftsman, and set it up in secret. And all the people shall say, Amen. Cursed is the one who treats his father or his mother with contempt ... Cursed is the one who moves his neighbor's landmark ... Cursed is the one who makes the blind to wander off the road ... Cursed is the one who perverts the justice due the stranger, the fatherless, and widow ... Cursed is the one who lies with his father's wife, because he has uncovered his father's bed.

Deuteronomy 27:26 says, "Cursed is the one who does not confirm all the words of this law. And all the people shall say, 'Amen.'"

Every curse has its own specific manifestation from the spiritual realms down to the natural. We find those manifestations further down in Deuteronomy 28:15–68. This entire passage expresses the consequences of breaking God's law. However, the most serious concern of the Lord has always been that of forsaking him and turning to other gods. But, as long as you people of God:

> Diligently obey the voice of the Lord your God, to observe carefully all His commandments which I command you today, that the Lord your God will set you high above all the nations of the earth. And all these blessings shall come upon you and overtake you (Deuteronomy 28:1–2).

Jesus emphasized on obedience as an expression of our love for him, no more as a burden or heavy weight to carry. John 14:15 says, "If you love me, keep my commandments." John 14:21 (NKJV), says, "He who has My commandments and keep them, it is he who loves me.

And he who loves Me will be loved by my Father, and I will love him and manifest Myself to him."

Jesus destroyed the curses on the cross and revealed himself to men by making possible that which was impossible to man. You will be amazed to see how the Lord will manifest himself to you and make it possible for you to abide in his word. As you learn to know him better and love him more and more one day at a time, remember that he first loved you. He was bruised for our iniquity. We deserved the punishment. The punishment for our peace was upon him. And, by his stripes, we are healed.

We are completely free and healed from all those curses because we believe in Jesus Christ and in the power of his word and unfailing love.

Importance of Blessing versus Cursing

The third of God's declaration of curse in the Scriptures appears when God begins to reveal himself to Abraham. In this context, God is bestowing blessings upon blessings on the man whom he is calling to further be the father of faith for God's children. One of the protective blessings and assurance of victory was that the Lord would curse those who curse Abraham.

We must know and understand our God and know who we are and what we have. This is why the phase of faith in the process of the accomplishment of salvation and all the blessings thereof should retain our attention in a peculiar manner.

The beginning of the revelation and knowledge of God is the starting point of the implementation of the divine plan of salvation as the Lord promised right after the fall of man into sin because of his great love.

When God dealt with Adam, Eve, and the devil, he cursed

the serpent and the ground, but protected the woman and her seed, saying her seed would bruise the head of that serpent. Two major entities are to be considered as remarkable. Now we can understand that they were signs of the coming of Christ the Savior and the works of salvation that would take place on Calvary with the final great victory in the resurrection of our Lord.

From the time when God drove Adam and Eve from Eden to the event of the cross, God took man of Earth through a process. The mysterious process in building or implementing his plan appears to be like bringing puzzles together. The first center puzzle in the building process was Abraham's walk with the Lord. When God remembers his promises, he shows up on time. He introduced himself as "the God of Abraham."

When the Lord God called him to a new promised land, he encouraged him by bestowing seven great blessings upon him.

> Genesis 12:1–3 (NKJV) says: Now the Lord had said to Abram: "Get out of your country, from your family and from your father's house, to a land that I will show you. I will make you a great nation; I will bless you and make your name great; and you shall be a blessing; I will bless those who bless you, and I will curse him who curses you; And in you all the families of the earth shall be blessed."

These blessings were not given to Abraham alone as an individual. God is also addressing his descendants and generations to come.

When I talk about another curse for cursing, I just want to draw the attention of the world to be very cautious in dealing with the children of the promise, that is, the children of Israel. They are the foundation of God's blessings on Earth. Those who fight against or mistreat the people of Israel are automatically under the curse of Gen 12:3 above.

> In Christ Jesus, we all are partakers of Abraham's blessings today. The Apostle Paul wrote an extraordinary revelation about our participation in or sharing of God's promise to Abraham for our knowledge and understanding. There is a mystery in the gospel of Jesus Christ that the Lord revealed. Ephesians 3:6 says: How that by revelation He made known to me the mystery, which in other ages was not made known to the sons of men as it has now been revealed by the Spirit to His holy apostles and prophets; that the Gentiles should be fellow heirs, of the same body, and partakers of His promise in Christ through the gospel.

Jesus is teaching us in Luke 6:27–28, "But I tell you who hear me: Love your enemies, do good to those who hate you. Bless those who curse you, pray for those who mistreat you."

As children of God, we must learn and apply forgiveness so our Heavenly Father may also forgive our trespasses and take care of every situation we encounter. In God's sight, we must appear like little children because the kingdom of heaven is reserved to those who are like infants.

I want you to know that, if anyone curses you, he will be cursed. But, as for you, the Lord says you should not curse. You should always give blessings and grace.

Jesus came and took those curses and death on the cross for you and me so we may reconcile with our Heavenly Father and gain victory over sin and its consequences that are infirmities, sickness, and diseases. "By his stripes, we are healed." So, by walking with him in victory, you will be qualified for sitting with him on his throne, just as he overcame sin and destroyed he who held the power of death (the devil) and sat at his father's throne. Our victory over death also gives us the assurance that he is coming back to judge the living and dead and we shall be with him forever.

Part III
Spiritual Warfare

Satan and Demons Are Real

Talking about demonic stronghold operations or demonology in general is a subject of an extremely wide exposition. This chapter will only condense important information confirmed with the Word of God, which will enlighten you on activities that take place in a world that the natural human eyes do not or cannot see. You would be surprised to hear that a large number of people do not believe in the existence of demons or unclean spirits and believe even less in their manifestations and control of human life and activities. As we read earlier about false biblical teachings, some churches have developed teachings on the nonexistence of the devil and evil spiritual beings and have succeeded in wiping this concept from their followers' minds, even though they see much evil around them. Right now, I pray for those skeptics who read this material to be delivered from the bondage and scales of ignorance and begin to dwell in the presence of the powerful Lord God Almighty.

It is extremely important to realize that every natural or

physical effect and manifestation has its cause or representation in the spiritual world or realm. You begin to realize that your thoughts or desires to commit such an action, conduct yourself in one manner or another, or desire to go (or not go) to one place when it is required are all under the control of either God for good, positiveness, and righteousness or satan for bad (evil), negativity, and destruction. Your own human will or personality will choose to go one way or the other. You are influenced, but the choice is still yours as for whom to obey. Forces of oppressions can essentially influence your will. Know that unseen forces control and influence your own personal thoughts or desires. We can understand these concepts when we willingly surrender to Jesus Christ and receive the gifts of the Holy Spirit, the Comforter, Leader, and Teacher of all true believers. The following passage is explicit, showing that the power of evil really influences man.

Romans 7:15–20 demonstrates clearly how we struggle in our daily life while trying to do good things or simply abide by the perfect will of God, all in vain.

> He says: "I do not understand what I do. For what I want to do I do not do, but what I hate I do. And if I do what I do not want to do, I agree that the law is good. As it is, It is no longer I myself who do it, but it is sin living in me. I know that nothing good lives in me, that is in my sinful nature (flesh). For I have the desire to do what is good, but I cannot carry it out. For what I do is not the good I want to do; no, the evil I do not want to do, this I keep on doing. Now if I do what I do not want to do, it is no longer I who do it, but it is sin living in me that does it."

This is a wonderful revelation. If I do what I do not want, it is not I who does it. Somebody must be doing it. He started his evil work on man at Eden. The sinful nature is the part of our being that receives or hears the voices and communicates with the serpent or devil. According to the above passage, the sin

living in me or flesh is the point of contact and communication with the spiritual forces of evil, whose influence on human will and choice of action is obviously strong.

I understood this passage of the Scriptures because God had delivered me from demonic oppressions when he called me from darkness into his marvelous light, filled me with the Holy Spirit, and graciously opened my heart and mind to comprehend the Scriptures. My life was completely transformed the moment I responded to the altar call and surrendered all to him. When Christ took over my heart, soul, and body, I realized everything I hated but still was doing were actually orchestrated by satan and his demonic forces of influence. I was subject to spiritual manipulation and unconscious of that aspect upon my character and behavior.

Let me state one of the many scenarios here to illustrate the above Bible quotation. I hated smoking, but I was a chain-smoker. I never took pleasure in it because I had reached the point of damaging my health. Nevertheless, I continued to swallow that nicotine day after day, hour after hour. My testimony or experience with Christ is extraordinary. Jesus said in Matt 19:26, "With man this is impossible, but with God all things are possible." No man can fight against those evil forces and succeed if God is not with him. However, we are more than conquerors through Christ Jesus who gives us strength through the indwelling Holy Spirit. This is why he says that, with God, all things are possible. We are the temples of God, according to 1Cor. 3:16; "Don't you know that you yourselves are God's temple and that God's Spirit lives in you?

I was born in a Christian family and attended church as I was being brought up. My mother, whose father was an elder of the Evangelical Church, grew up fearing and revering the Lord. She led me step-by-step to the path of church activities and taught me how to pray and, much more, never to miss church services on Sundays. But, during my high school age, far away from the family, I began to mingle with club friends, drinking and smoking, going to parties, and more. Before I realized it, I was not going to church anymore. Even less was I interested in God's matters. Several years later, despite the fact I had completed my education and had an above middle-class position in society, my life was a mess. I was a chain-smoker. The only time I was not smoking was when I was asleep. Someone would say, "Why do you smoke so much? When are you going to stop? You always say you hate smoking. You know you are destroying yourself." I would answer, "Yes, I know. I really want to stop this nasty thing, but I just can't." This is just one of the strongholds that Jesus delivered me from. He healed my body. Because I know where he brought me from, I do not and cannot play with his salvation. Jesus Christ suffered so much for my deliverance that I cannot take it for granted. What he did for me is priceless. The same is my desire and prayer for all who do not have the knowledge of the only begotten Son of God.

He brought me out of darkness of ignorance and sorrow, out of all the pain that the lack of knowledge can cause. He counts me now among his chosen people. What a blessing to be especially chosen by God! 1 Peter 2:9-10 says, "But you are a chosen people, a royal priesthood, a holy nation, a people belonging to God, that you may declare the praises of Him who called you out of darkness into His wonderful light. Once you were not a people, but now you are the people of God;..."

The man who led me to Christ Jesus first showed me how I was under the control of demonic forces operating in the air. I was desperate without God. I was seeking solutions to a messed-up life that apparently seemed not to be restorable. In fact, I was so hopeless and miserable that, like a ripe sweet fruit ready to be eaten, I listened to him with awe, ready to be invaded by the power of the word of Christ and his anointing of healing and deliverance.

As he was talking to me that afternoon on a day that seemed gloomy, lifting up his Bible, and pointing the book to my face, he repeated many times, "Only Jesus Christ can set you free from those forces." Each time he pronounced "Jesus Christ," I felt like a blow on my chest was creating sparks all over my body. I realized I was a slave. It is true that you are slave to whoever you obey. I was obeying the devil and destroying my own life. As he was talking, I began to see myself like in a giant screen with my entire life laid bare. I began to feel hatred growing progressively in my heart. Hatred was directed against me, as seen in the screen where I could see the ugliness of my life and against all those evil forces around me. Then I saw satan in all my past life. I saw him in that cigarette. I saw him in that alcohol and the nightclubs, swinging with women around. I saw him in all sexual immoralities. I saw him burning all the monies I had earned and lying and laughing after throwing my life in a muddy gutter. I saw the chain of bondage around my neck and shackles at my arms and ankles. I was speechless all the time. He ended his speech, saying, "I thank God for what he has just done. I have prayed for months that he give me the opportunity and word to tell you all this." He gave me a small piece of paper with a church address and pastor's name written on it. He advised me to go there for prayer. That was it. He did not pray for me, but he had accomplished his mission.

This man who just spoke about Jesus with extraordinary conviction and boldness was my own young brother, who had sought the Lord and received him a year earlier in Paris. That afternoon, he was returning to France, very happy to have fulfilled a mission for the glory of God. Right after this encounter, I began to cry out to the Lord. I cried for days and weeks until, one day about two months later, I stood alone before the altar call at a nightly church service and finally received my Lord and Savior Jesus Christ as Lord of my entire life, the wonderful Prince of Peace and deliverer and healer of my soul. I received him fully deep in my soul and spirit and gave him all my body, talents, knowledge, and desires as I declared, "Lord, I want you to do what you want with me and make me be what you want me to be." He made clay out of me and became my glorious potter to this day. My conversion was awesome. Signs and wonders, spiritual deliverance, and physical healing followed. I became my pastor's servant, like Elisha was to Elijah, until, one day, the Lord spoke to me while I was interceding for my friends and family. "I called you for this very purpose … I will manifest my power in your life … See, I am sending you to the world to deliver my people from bondage." God is faithful. To him be all the glory.

I know this situation of bondage happens to millions of people, even believers around the world, in many different areas of their lives or activities. We do what we hate. We cannot what we want to do. An outside force is operating in us or through us. This situation is automatically true for any person who does not know God. The world is fighting and perishing because of lack of knowledge. It is also unfortunately true for church people, especially a large number of believers today.

Many come to Christ and are churchgoers, but they still live in bondage. It is important to be aware of this truth. You have to know the truth before you can be set free from satanic bondage. If you are not aware of these facts, your life will be a mess when the negative forces lead you from the spiritual realms. Many people that the Scriptures describe as witches or sorcerers work directly with those evil spirits to develop spiritual strength and power. Those people have the capability to dominate others or even influence the thoughts and minds of the weak ones. People who practice witchcraft or voodoo do so by communicating with evil spirits. They have developed the capability to perform miraculous signs and wonders just to deceive the ignorant people. The result of their miraculous performances is demonic possession, various plagues, and death. The only way out is deliverance by the power of God.

We are under pressures and stresses and struggle with circumstances on a daily basis. We even fight our fellow brothers, friends, or co-workers, not knowing we all have one common enemy.

Ephesians 6:10–12 says, "Finally, be strong in the Lord and in His mighty power. Put on the full armor of God so that you can take your stand against the devil's schemes. For our struggle is not against flesh and blood, but against the rulers, against the authorities, against the powers of this dark world and against the spiritual forces of evil in the heavenly realms."

Who Is Satan?

This chapter could be the title and subject of an entire book, due to its importance and especially urgent necessity of all faithful believers of Christ Jesus to comprehend who we are as children of God in what kind of spirito-universe we are evaluating. Acquiring the knowledge of spiritual matters will help more to overcome the daily battle against this world of darkness so we can respond with victory to the critical calls from our Lord as addressed to the seven churches of Asia. In Revelation chapters 2 and 3, you will find these calls seven times. "To him who overcomes I will ... (or) ... He who overcomes shall ..." Jesus promises great rewards to those who will overcome.

How can we overcome issues or anything we are ignorant of? Can we imagine how many people in the church are perishing because of ignorance and/or lack of knowledge?

The encounter of Lucifer gives us a legitimate explanation of satan's origin and reasons of wickedness in the world thereof.

These passages from Isaiah and Ezekiel render the account more clearly than ever.

> Isaiah 14:11–14 says: All your pomp has been brought down to the grave, along with the noise of your harps; maggots are spread out beneath you and worms cover you. How you have fallen from heaven, o morning star, son of the dawn! You have been cast down to the earth, you who once laid low the nations! You said in your heart, "I will ascend to heaven; I will raise my throne above the stars of God. I will sit enthroned on the mount of assembly, on the utmost heights of the sacred mountain. I will ascend above the tops of the clouds; I will make myself like the most high."

Isaiah 14:15 tells Lucifer where his end is going to be after the return of Jesus Christ, the King of kings and Lord of lords, coming back in glory and power. "But you are brought down to the grave, to the depths of the pit."

Revelation 20:10 tells about this final fall into the lake of fire for eternity. It says, "And the devil, who deceived them, was thrown into the lake of burning sulfur, where the beast and the false prophet had been thrown. They will be tormented day and night for ever and ever."

> Ezekiel 28:12–15 says: You were the model of perfection, full of wisdom and perfect in beauty. You were in Eden, the garden of God; every precious stone adorned you: ruby, topaz and emerald, chrysolite, onyx and jasper, sapphire, turquoise and beryl. Your settings and mountings were made of gold; on the day you were

> created they were prepared. You were anointed as a guardian cherub, for so I ordain you. You were on the holy mount of God; you walked among the fiery stones. You were blameless in your ways from the day you were created till wickedness was found in you.

Every person who is aware of spiritual matters must know that satan is at the head of this present world system. Although our physical eyes don't see him, he was the real invisible power behind the successive world rulers of Tyra, Babylon, Persia, Greece, Rome, and many more. Recently, we can still remember Hitler and Mussolini, who had openly incarnated satan in all his wickedness. Satan has been implementing his aims of being god through world rulers. Most of them claimed to be gods, such as the pharaoh of Egypt, the emperor of Rome, and so forth.

As we are giving the spiritual warfare a serious examination, we understand satan is the number one enemy of man and of Yeshua Hamashiach the Son of God. This is why he has a deep hatred toward God's children. He massacred the believers in the first century. When he saw the blood of the martyrs were fertilizing the worldwide field of the gospel, he changed the tactics, sent demons in the form of men into the churches, who masqueraded as angels of light, and turned the disciples away from the authentic truth and teaching of Jesus Christ and the apostles thereafter.

> Paul foresaw one of the sad victories satan had over the church people (not the church as body of Christ), and he was very concerned when he kept sending warnings to the churches. We still have those warnings with us today, but we are not paying attention. Acts 20:28–31 says: Keep watch over yourselves and all the flocks

of which the Holy Spirit has made you overseers. Be shepherds of the Church of God, which He bought with his own blood. I know that after I leave, savage wolves will come in among you and will not spare the flock. Even from your own number men will arise and distort the truth in order to draw away disciples after them.

This warning is truer now than ever before. In fact, we lost our appellation of "disciple" that Jesus gave us numerous times. The Roman power took over the leadership of the church and imposed the name "Christian." So Christianity brought in pagan religion rituals and ways of worshipping idols instead of the Lord. The Holy Spirit was forgotten. Finally, the manifestation of the power of God in healing and deliverance was denied. When we study the church of Jesus Christ, as operated by the Holy Spirit in the first ten chapters of the Acts of the Apostles, we are urged to shed a tear at what we see or what we have today.

I thank God for what he has done when he showed up again at Azusa Street in 1906. It is true that the Lord is faithful. He promised that, before the end, he would restore all things. The world witnessed a brand-new move of the Holy Spirit after so many centuries that the church had been asleep. I'd rather say "dead." Satan was the chief musician and an extraordinarily bright instrumentalist in heaven, also occupying the position of cherub angel. These angels stand right beside God. When Lucifer's pride burst out, he deceived one-third of the angels and fell with them on this atmospheric sphere. Jude 6 states, "And the angels who did not keep their positions of authority but abandoned their own home—these he has kept in darkness, bound with everlasting chains for judgment on the great day."

These angel followers of satan are the great number of demons at his service who are bothering us every time and everywhere, outside and inside the church. They attack us in many ways, including: Projecting bad thought; Working hard to mess up our minds, which are their battlefields; Developing hatred among brethren, families, or co-workers; Gossiping through our mouths and turning marriages upside down.

Evil spirits are managers of most diseases. Witches and members of witchcraft organizations use them and send them to operate against individuals, families, and communities. They are invisible smokers, drinkers, drug addicts, adulterers, and liars behind the people who practice them. They send and manage diseases in human bodies. Demonic strongholds provoke and manage heart attacks, ulcers, AIDS, barrenness, miscarriages, and so forth. Their job is to enter your life without invitation just to steal your joy, peace, money, job, family, and happiness. They are there to kill and to destroy. In John 10:10, the Lord says, "The thief does not come except to steal, and to kill, and to destroy. I have come that they may have life, and that they may have it more abundantly." (NKJV)

Demonic organizations led by satan are our common enemy. This is not to be taken for granted. Let us be constantly conscious that our adversaries, the devil and his evil spirits of darkness, are roaming around every day, seeking someone to devour. So it is necessary to know your enemy, understand his strategy, and study his territories, war plans, and weapons. At the same time, it is also necessary to know who you are, know the Lord your God, understand God's strategy and plans for you, and stand firm.

Physical warfare and bloodshed are described in their full reality in the Bible. Satan wants to produce the downfall of man, no matter what tactics he uses to reach his satisfaction. He may introduce himself softly and gently, like he did to Eve, but beware. He will kill you as softly as he comes. He is referred to as the thief in John 10:10.

We have to be aware that satan has a government, army, and billions of demonic strongholds in the air, on Earth, and under Earth. He has churches that are totally under his control. He has prophets, doctors, teachers, and pastors totally under his control, all working for him. All the satanic organizations in the spiritual realms form what we call "powers of darkness." Satan is the king or overall boss of all the powers of darkness, including their human servants, sorcerers, or witchcraft practitioners. Their job in this world is only to harm and respond to God's desire to send plagues or disasters when God deems it necessary to send punishment and destruction to the rebellious people.

These rebellious themselves belong to or were deceived by the same satan. The powers of darkness are wicked spirits; they are envying and jealous and always ready to and seeking to put men in trouble. Their human agents are likewise. All the troubles and desperate situations we see or experience in the world, at all levels, are either created or just cleverly managed by satan and his demonic organizations, which include his human agents. Even when God decides to destroy or kill someone or people, satan will rush before the throne and ask to carry out the sentence. The good angels of God are love and compassionate. They don't want to harm. They praise God and manifest joy when the sinner repents and turns to God. The following passage of the Scriptures demonstrates the schemes and evil characteristic of the devil.

In 1 King 22, we learn how satan went to the throne of God to receive permission to kill King Ahab, who had terribly displeased the Lord with his wife Jezebel.

> For three years there was no war between Aram and Israel. But in the third year Jehoshaphat king of Judah went down to see the king of Israel. The king of Israel had said to his officials, "Don't you know that Ramoth Gilead belongs to us and yet we are doing nothing to retake it from the king of Aram?"
>
> So he asked Jehoshaphat, "Will you go with me to fight against Ramoth Gilead?"

Jehoshaphat replied to the king of Israel, "I am as you are, my people as your people, my horses as your horses." But Jehoshaphat also said to the king of Israel, "First seek the counsel of the Lord." King Jehoshaphat reminded King Ahab that, before you engage into such battle, project it has to come from the Lord. This was a time when the king of Israel had turned his back to the Lord. The entire story of Ahab is about evil, idolatry, and murder of God's prophets. First Kings 21:25 says, "There was never a man like Ahab, who sold himself to do evil in the eyes of the Lord, urged by Jezebel his wife." Ahab's life was totally under the control of satan, whose goal and inner desire are to destroy man made in the image of God.

In his part of the kingdom, Jehoshaphat was a commendable king. The Lord was with him because, in his early years, he walked in the ways of his father, David. God gave him extraordinary victories in battles and blessed his kingdom. But, unlike Jehoshaphat, there was no place for the Lord in Ahab's heart. If the Lord is not in your heart and if the Holy Spirit does not lead you, you will automatically serve the desire or walk in the schemes of satan.

First Kings 22:6–8 says:

> So the king of Israel brought together the prophets—about four hundred men—and asked them, "Shall I go to war against Ramoth Gilead, or shall I refrain?" "Go," they answered, "for the Lord will give it into the king's hand." But Jehoshaphat asked, "Is there not a prophet of the Lord here whom we can inquire of?" The king of Israel answered Jehoshaphat, "There is one man through whom we can inquire of the Lord, but I hate him because he never prophesies anything good about me, but always bad. He is Micaiah, son of Imlah." "The king should not say that," Jehoshaphat replied.

Jehoshaphat persuaded Ahab because he knew Jezebel's prophets were all liars. They were not true prophets of the Lord. They were saying only what the king wanted to hear. We will now learn that demonic strongholds were manipulating and projecting their lies.

> First Kings 22:17–22 says: Then Micaiah answered, "I saw all Israel scattered on the hills like sheep without a shepherd," and the Lord said, "These people have no master. Let each one go home in peace." The king of Israel said to Jehoshaphat, "Didn't I tell you he never prophesies anything good about me, but only bad?" Micaiah continued, "Therefore hear the word of the Lord: I saw the Lord sitting on His throne with all the host of heaven standing around Him on His right and

on His left." And the Lord said, "Who will entice Ahab into attacking Ramoth Gilead and going to his death there?" One suggested this, and another that. Finally, a spirit came forward, stood before the Lord and said, "I will entice him." "By what means?" the Lord asked.

"I will go out and be a lying spirit in mouths of all his prophets," he said.

"You will succeed in enticing him," said the Lord. "Go and do it."

So now the Lord has put a lying spirit in the mouths of all these prophets of yours. The Lord has decreed disaster for you.

The lying spirit could be an agent of satan, an evil spirit sent by God to condemn Ahab and his false prophets in their sins. Their hearts were so hardened to the truth that God finally had to get rid of them after turning the hearts of the Israelites back to him during the Mount Carmel encounter between Elijah and the eight hundred and fifty false prophets.

Idolatry, the worship of any other gods but the Lord God Almighty, went rampant in Israel as acts of disobedience to the Lord's command.

When we observe the actions of satan throughout the Scriptures and in the world today, he is extremely smart in imitating what God does in order to deceive men. He has churches, doctors, pastors, and others who fake religious manifestations. He comes to those who seek or love God, masquerading as an angel of light. He always wants to be God. He has made himself the god of this present world. He knows his time is near and his works and activities are soon ending. He is so jealous and sick to see men saved by grace and through faith in Jesus Christ that his primary goal is to lead as many as he can. Why not the whole mankind (if he could)? To hell with him. He knows that, as God has decreed, his end is the lake of fire for eternity. This is why he uses all types of tricks to deceive men.

When I talked about the origin of diseases, it all began with satan deceiving Adam and Eve and tricking them to disobey the instruction of God and Creator. He still uses the same tricks today.

It is important to develop the sense of discernment and know and recognize the works of the devil. This is how we can also learn through the guidance of the Holy Spirit in order to avoid any damage to our spiritual connection with God.

Spiritual Warfare

Spiritual warfare is referred to as fight, combat, or wrestling that takes place between men and the spirits of darkness or demonic strongholds that are operating in the heavenly and earthly realms. In fact, we humankind are undergoing constant battles throughout our existence. This is well-spoken of in Eph 6:11–12 (NKJV): "Put on the whole armor of God, that you may be able to stand against the wiles of the devil. For we do not wrestle against flesh and blood, but against principalities, against powers, against the rulers of the darkness of this age, against spiritual hosts of wickedness in the heavenly places."

Those spirits are well-organized, just like an army or government, and they are subject to a supreme chief well-known as satan or the devil. We learn he has always waged war or tried to fight against the Lord. Also knowing he cannot dare to succeed in any battle planned against God directly, he continually attacks the people of God to hurt God's heart. He knows that, by attacking the children of God, he is provoking God directly. The Scriptures tell us that God has engraved his children in his hand. Isaiah 49:16, "See, I have engraved you on the palms of my hands..."

The devil began to wage war in heaven before he was thrown down on the then-dark and formless Earth. I believe he was extremely angry and full of hatred when he saw the creation occurring around him and when God made man in the image of himself. Satan was very jealous when he heard God tell the man to be fruitful, subdue Earth, and rule over every living creature that moves on the ground.

Oh, I can imagine that mad serpent saying to himself, "What? They are not satisfied to have thrown us down here. Now they have made a living being out of the dust and told him to rule over us? We shall see. We're not going to let that work." Think about that. This is where warfare against man began. The major intrinsic characters of satan are wickedness, hatred, jealousy, lying, and every imaginable bad things that originated from these four.

The serpent saw this man was walking in the glory of God. He waited for the proper time to execute his first Machiavellian plan of downfall of man unto death. He was hoping Adam and Eve would literally die when they obeyed him and disobeyed God. Unfortunately for him, it appeared that God is love, his mercy endures forever, and he made us to be his sons and daughters eternally.

In the course of sentencing the serpent and the woman, God set up a mysterious plan of salvation that Adam and Eve did not understand at all. Genesis 3:15 says, "And I will put enmity between you and the woman, and between your offspring and hers; he will crush your head, and you will strike his heel."

Due to satan's origin as a former heavenly angel, he has a strong character of cleverness and intelligence. He understood this mysterious prophetic sentence that was foretelling the Golgotha victory of our Redeemer and the beginning of his own eternal doom. Since then, he also repeatedly set up plans to try to stop the coming of the Lord. But who can comprehend the deep wisdom and unsearchable ways of the Lord's thoughts?

Satan also set up a plan of destruction against the children of God: Demons began to possess the first man born on Earth, Cain. He was jealous and filled with hatred. When he saw Abel had pleased the Lord with his offerings, he killed him.

In his great wisdom, God waited nearly five hundred years after the flood to lay down the foundation of the works of the cross with the call of Abraham. The evil one heard God blessing and sending Abraham to a special land. Genesis 12:2–3 says, "I will make you into a great nation and I will bless you. I will make your name great, and you will be a blessing. I will bless those who bless you, and whoever curses you I will curse; and all the peoples on earth will blessed through you."

Note the importance of Gen 12:7. "The Lord appeared to Abram and said, 'To your offspring I will give this land.'" God kept blessing and talking about the offspring.

The devil thought by killing Abel, he had killed the offspring God spoke about to Eve. Now there is another promise of the offspring with Abraham. Sarai was barren. But, before she conceived, satan tried to mess up her womb. So he rushed to Egypt, entered in Pharaoh's heart, organized with his demon forces to draw Abraham out of Canaan to Egypt, and declared that Sarai was his sister. Pharaoh took Sarai to be his wife. Thank God. He always intervenes on our behalf. O Lord, you are always right on time. Pharaoh got threatened to death because of Abraham's wife, so he sent them away with great riches. Praise the Lord.

These plans are more aimed continuously at destroying God's plan for man. Jacob's life was overwhelmed with trials. He went through various attacks, long-sufferings, and pains before he brought forth the upcoming twelve tribes of Israel.

These plans include Joseph threatening life during his youth and satan trying to kill him in order to stop God's plan revealed through awesome dreams.

All these attacks and plan to destroy the chosen ones of God were aiming at diverting or stopping God's promise for salvation. The purpose of the war waged was precisely to prevent the coming of the Savior of mankind. But who can stop God from executing his will?

Isaiah 40:8 says, "But the word of our God stands forever." Isaiah 43:13 says, "Yes and from the ancient days I am He. No one can deliver out of my hand. When I act, who can reverse it?"

While God has plan for your prosperity and happiness, satan has a plan for your failure, disaster, and/or death. Knowing his time is near, he wants to draw as many people to him as possible.

All the pains and rebellion, wars, and downfalls that the children of Israel went through were orchestrated and operated by satan and his evil forces of darkness. From the slavery in Egypt to the worship of the golden calf in the wilderness, satan was the master planner. He grumbled against Moses in the wilderness, causing him to make mistake at the rock of Meriba. He inspired ten of the twelve spies who came back from exploring the promised land to discourage the people, creating unbelief amidst shouts of rebellion and causing them to wander forty years in the desert.

He introduced idolatry in Israel to its highest level, with the worship of Baal, the asherah poles, and many other abominations. He succeeded in turning Israel completely from the ways of the

Lord their God. The people provoked God to anger, but the pathway to Golgotha could not be fathomed because God's mercy and love were constantly hovering over Earth.

The greatest battle of all times and the mightiest victory on our behalf was that of the cross and from the resurrection to the ascension of the King of kings and Lord of lords. This is testified by our Lord himself in Rev 1:17–18: When I saw Him, I fell at His feet as though dead. Then He placed His right hand on me and said: "Do not be afraid. I am the First and the Last. I am the Living One; I was dead, and behold I am alive for ever and ever! And I hold the keys of death and Hades."

Jesus died on the cross, not only for our sins, but to fulfill the promise of healing and deliverance that everybody in the Church knows. Isaiah 53:5 (KJV) says, "[A]nd with His stripes we are healed."

At this particular time, we are blessed to witness the event of the end-times. We see many biblical prophecies being fulfilled to our hearing. Therefore, the Spirit of the Lord is calling for more awareness because satan is actively busy. He knows his time is near. He and his army of darkness and all the wicked people who followed him, served him, and worshiped him shall be thrown in the pit of perdition forever. The major purpose of his fight is to deceive as many people as possible and take them to hell with him.

Blessed be the name of the Lord our God and Savior Jesus Christ who has blessed us with spiritual gifts in order to draw us to the place where he would graciously reveal himself to us. He drew Moses to the wilderness. He drew Saul to the desert before allowing him to enter the city of Damascus to experience the power of salvation. We are all drawn one way or the other to a type of wilderness, where we receive the revelation of the Son of the Living God. Jesus said, "No one knows the Son except the Father, and no one knows the Father except the Son, and those to whom the Son chooses to reveal him" (Matt 11:27).

It is important to realize that the knowledge of God and the understanding of his word and works are revealed. One day,

Jesus asked his disciples, "Who do people say the Son of man is?" (Matt 16). They gave different answers. Some say you are Elijah; some say you are one of the prophets. "But what about you?" he asked. "Who do you say I am?"

At that particular time, Jesus had not yet told his disciples that he was the savior the Israelites were waiting for, as foretold by the prophets. The people were thinking and saying, "He could also be a great prophet, like Moses or Elijah." To his last question, Peter stood and said, "You are the Christ, the Son of the Living God." Jesus replied. "Blessed are you, Simon son of Jonah, for this was not revealed to you by man, but by my Father in heaven" (Matt 16: 13–17).

The word of God is revealed, and the operations of its power are effective by gift. The knowledge of the son of man and healing power through his name are not acquired from bible colleges or universities. There is nothing wrong about colleges or universities. It is even recommended to acquire and increase academic knowledge. It is very good for our social and intellectual development, but it is far from being the condition to receive the understanding of the mystery of God, which only he reveals to those he chooses to reveal. The Holy Spirit distributes those gifts to each one just as he pleases.

This is why a great number of church people have no clue of

the manifestations of spiritual strongholds in their lives and even their health. It is true that the majority of believers today serve the Lord wholeheartedly, participating in various church programs and meetings, making tremendous donations, and staying faithful with their tithes, but you see them struggling day after day and year after year, praying to God for healing. Nothing or very little would happen. But you can still find some few men and women of God today who have sought the Lord from the deepest part of their hearts, and they are walking with the Almighty with fear and trembling, out of respect, obedience, and foolish faith. Men and women of God, especially in areas where satan operates powerfully through sorcerers or witch organizations, are conscious of the spiritual warfare the church of Jesus Christ is undergoing. They have made themselves available to be prayer warriors. These are anointed to demolish the strongholds, heal the brokenhearted, and establish God's earthly spiritual army.

We are subjected to spiritual wars all around us, even though we encounter them in the natural realm. The physical wars in the natural realms are completely operated from the spiritual realms. The Bible states that we (the believers) are spiritual in Christ Jesus, if the Spirit of Christ dwells in us. 1 Corinthians 2:6–10 says, "We do however, speak a message of wisdom among the mature, but not the wisdom of this age, which are coming to nothing. No, we speak of God's secret wisdom that has been hidden and that God destined for our glory before time began. None of the rulers of this age understood it, for if they had, they would not have crucified the Lord of glory. However, as it is written:

No eye has seen,
No ear has heard,
No mind has conceived
What god has prepared for those who love Him.
But God has revealed it to us by His Spirit.
The Spirit searches all things, even the deep
things of God."

1 Corinthians 2:14–16 says, "The man without the Spirit does not accept the things that come from the Spirit of God, for they are foolishness to him, and he cannot understand them because they are spiritually discerned. The spiritual man makes judgments about all things, but he himself is not subject to any man's judgment: For who has known the mind of the Lord that he may instruct Him? But we have the mind of Christ."

The "rulers of this age" refers exactly to satan and his government.

It is so wonderful that we who were lost in this world of darkness, stumbling here and there like sheep without shepherd, after we had come to the knowledge of the Son of God and received the Spirit and mind of Christ, we can also discern spiritual existence and its impacts in the natural realm.

To God be the Glory.

Part IV
The Solution and Testimony Of Yeshua Hamashiach

God's Promise for Health and Healing

The story of the exodus of the children of Israel from Egypt contains such extraordinary scenarios that it takes being an unwavering Bible believer to apprehend those spectacular events. The miracles, signs, and wonders God performed with Moses were aiming at introducing himself to the world and making himself known as the Almighty, Most High above all the gods of the peoples, Creator of all things visible and invisible, and Living God. At this point of time, he had revealed his existence only to quiet patriarchs, including Noah, Abraham, Rebecca, Jacob, and so forth. Now the Lord was about to exit six hundred thousand men, without counting the women and children, out of bondage and out of Egypt, together with cattle, herds, and all their belongings. This move is still unique in its kind in the entire history of mankind.

The plagues that hit the land of Egypt prior to the exodus, the great redemptive event of the crossing of the Red Sea, and other extraordinary divine interventions have provoked a large amount of skepticism in the modern society. Even some church people partially believe what the Scriptures contain, and this is mainly the obstacle to their faith in the fullness of the divine power.

As I develop this chapter, I want to emphasize two major issues: the level of our belief and firmness of the faith that generates its substance. I cannot say how many times I have read the Torah, but, every time I happen to cross over Exodus 7 to 14, I am overwhelmed with increasing fascination. The way we receive God's move and power through the Word as rightly divided and our commitment and determination in walking right with him will make a complete difference.

I am talking here about God's promise for health. Why should we children of God encounter more sicknesses and diseases in the church? Sadly, not believing the divine healing power, we put our trust more in physicians and medications. That never solved the problems the way God would solve them for us. I hope this chapter, by the Lord's grace, will bring the answer to help bring our determining faith and project to our understanding.

After the crossing of the Red Sea, two important manifestations took place. Picture yourself being there in the midst of the Israelites, walking between two high walls of water in a sea, as on a dry land, practically all night with a spectacular pillar of fire producing bright light for them to see. First, they were in awe and terrifically astounded. Exodus 14:30–31 says, "That day the Lord saved Israel from the hands of the Egyptians, and Israel saw the Egyptians lying dead on the shore. And when the Israelites saw the great power of the Lord displayed against the

Egyptians, the people feared the Lord and put their trust in Him and in Moses his servant."

Right after they saw all these wonders, they organized a praise and worship party by the seashore where the Egyptians and their horses were lying dead with broken war chariots scattered. Psalms 20:7 says, "Some trust in chariots and some in horses, but we trust in the name of the Lord. They are brought to their knees and fall, but we rise up and stand firm." First they praised the Lord after witnessing his wonderful deeds.

The second manifestation took place three days later as they were walking in the desert toward their dream destination. As they were thirsty, they lost control of their faith in God, who had just demonstrated he could do anything for their well-being. They grumbled.

The first time the Lord God spoke after Israel's baptism through the red sea, it was to promise health and healing.

> Exodus 15:25–26 (KJV) says: There He made for them a statute and an ordinance, and there He proved them, And said, "If thou wilt diligently hearken to the voice of the Lord thy God, and wilt do that which is right in his sight, and wilt give ear to his commandments, and keep all his statutes, I will put none of these diseases upon thee, which I have brought upon the Egyptians: for I am the Lord that healeth thee."

The New Testament is the fulfillment of all God's promises since Adam, manifested by Christ's death on the cross, his resurrection, and ascension to heaven. We are saved by God's grace through faith in Yeshua the Messiah. We confirm the completion of our salvation by engaging to follow Christ into the water of baptism as a symbol of conforming to his death and resurrection. We learn that, when we are saved, the Lord snatches us from the powers of darkness into his marvelous light, heading from the world of sin into his glorious kingdom.

The Old Testament is the type of the New Testament accomplishment. Our salvation today is well-pictured in this event. The slavery of the people of Israel, their mighty deliverance from Egypt, the Passover night followed by the crossing of the Red Sea, and the progress to the Promise Land is all picturing our life with Christ.

Egypt is the type of the world where we were enslaved by the devil and his demonic strongholds and bound by sinful nature without the knowledge of God. We gave our lives to the Lord, who brought us out of the world (Egypt). We got the baptism. The first voice we heard (and did not pay attention to) was that of the loving and caring father who does not want his children to be sick. The previous verses came to us one way or the other. God has addressed his merciful healing to us, and we might or might not have apprehended it. Nevertheless, note the promise for health and healing God gave was conditional. To this day, it still is.

It is very true that we can be healthy and strong all the days of our lives. I am writing this book by God's grace. He commanded and confirmed me to do so because of the testimony he graciously granted me, including renewal of life, youth, strength, and much more. Isaiah 40:28–31 says: "Do you not know? Have you not heard? The Lord is the everlasting God, the Creator of the ends of the earth. He will not grow tired or weary, and his understanding no one can fathom. He gives strength to the weary, and increases the power of the weak. Even youths grow tired and weary, and young men stumble and fall; but those who hope in the Lord will renew their strength, they will soar on wings like eagles, they will run and not grow weary, they will walk and not be faint." It is wonderful that salvation is not just of the soul. In fact, we are saved body and soul all together. The fundamental issue of every man on Earth is health. Oh, how sad and distressful it is when a person's health is deteriorated. His strength vanishes like smoke. He cannot work, and he is lying down in wait for others to take care of him. It is terrible to see a large number of people outside looking apparently well, but they live on unbearable medications and painkillers, breathing machines, blood-cleansing systems, and so forth. Again, the fundamental issue of every man on Earth, his hope and his most burning desire, is to be in good health and strong.

When the crowds were following Yeshua, it was because he was providing direct and total health solution. The Bible states in many passages that they were all healed. No one person on Earth is supposed to come to Christ and remain the same week after week and month after month in the church. I call that against the scriptural truth. Second Corinthians 5:17 (KJV) says, "Therefore, if any man be in Christ, he is a new creature; old things are passed away; behold, all things are become new..."

All things become new, and the most important thing for God is to be your loving father in your health. Your health must become new. If you were already healthy, get healthier. If your body is not saved or has not become new, I am taking no risk to ask if your soul has.

Salvation is taken so much for granted today by religious church people and their followers that you really wonder if all these crowds do understand what Christ the Redeemer is all about.

I want to assure you that Jesus is all about healing, deliverance, restoration, renewal, and constant victory battle against the world. It is not supposed to be otherwise.

> I was privileged to meet two honorable servants of the Lord whose lives have been endangered in the mission field where the Lord has been sending them to for the past fifteen years. Peter and Christine Darg are spreading the gospel of the Lord Jesus Christ to the Muslim people of the Middle East with extraordinary divine manifestations. Christine's testimonial book, *Miracles Among Muslims*, in which she is crying out to the Lord for the restoration of the authentic move of the Holy Spirit in the church, fascinated me.

"Dreams and visions should characterize the Spirit-filled life. This is the time of the revival of exploits, of mighty works, characterized by acts similar to those accomplished by biblical heroes. The Church desperately needs the supernatural, especially since Jesus Himself prophesied in Matt 24:24 that in the Last Days false christs and false prophets will demonstrate "great signs and wonders."

Satan will increasingly promote lying wonders and falsehoods … We should petition the Lord for greater discernment and for genuine miracles from God (164)."

I thank the Lord so much for Sister Christine for her outstanding book and especially for her cry for the restoration of the genuine power of the Holy Spirit in the church of God today as she recalls the biblical heroes' achievements. God's grace has led Christine to hit the right target. I have met very few people with that same spirit of concern and divine knowledge.

That was the burden the Lord graciously put on my heart since 1990. In a dream, I was observing on one side a devastated church full of lies, immorality, personal ambition, and greediness. On the other side, I was projected two thousand years back, watching the early church (that I called "primitive church") with Peter, John, Philip, Paul, and others operating in the fullness of God's anointing. Then I began to cry, asking the Lord, "Where is the primitive church?" After I woke up, I felt like a heavy load was inside my chest. I began to travel the city, going from church to church and seeking the primitive type of church in vain. About a year later, the Lord manifested himself to me again with similar dream and day vision, this time with more intensity. He increased the burden for the restoration of the church, prophesied six centuries before the victory of Golgotha. My cry and question was again, "Where is the primitive church, Lord?" What happened here will be disclosed at the proper time. I am going to bring this terrific story in my next book, *Believe Your Vision*.

God will do to you and for you exactly what you believe and confess. When you walk with him, it is a plus, and he will perfect your desire and faith to his utmost glory.

Many criteria needed to be added to the puzzle in order to obtain the clear view of the solution to human health problem. We must all agree that, in the beginning, was the Word who created all things and made man in the image of God. Therefore, in the beginning, God did not make man with sickness, illness, weakness, cripples, and/or death. All these came as consequences of the sin of disobedience. Romans 6:23 says, "For the wages of sin is death, but the gift of God is eternal life in Christ Jesus."

I am going to break down part of the puzzle of Exodus 15:26 (KJV). God has promised health and healing. But it is under four important conditions that the promise can be fully received and enjoyed. These conditions are very important to be understood because nobody can walk around them and reap the fruit thereof.

1. "If thou wilt diligently hearken to the voice of the Lord thy God." We must listen carefully to the voice of the Lord. If you are a layperson in God's affairs and cannot hear him for yourself, you can hear him through the preacher, pastor, teacher, or brethren who shares God's grace with you. So there is no excuse. When we gave our lives to Jesus and received him as Lord of our lives, we had heard the message with trust. We did not come to Jesus unconsciously. So we must listen diligently and pay close attention to what he is saying so we do not miss a dot.
2. "And wilt do that which is right in His sight." Now, after having listened carefully, knowing what is right in his sight, we ought to take action of obedience immediately. We must do what he says. He expects our acts of obedience, just like any father from his children. Is it not obvious?

"And wilt give ears to his commandments." Giving ears to God's commandments keeps us from falling in sin. "Do not lead us into temptation, but deliver us from evil." Temptation is a spirit that

3. roams around people. His evil mission is to push us or draw us to sin. A typical biblical example is that of King David the first time he did not give ears to God to go to war. He

fell with Bathsheba and murdered her husband. This story remained the saddest one throughout David's kingdom. For this reason, he prayed many times in Ps 119:11. "I have hidden your Word in my heart that I might not sin against you." Psalms 119:32–37 says, "I run in the path of your commands, for you have set me free. Teach me, O Lord, to follow your decrees; then I will keep them to the end. Give me understanding, and I will keep your law and obey it with all my heart. Direct me in the path of your commands, for there I find delight. Turn my heart toward your statutes and not toward selfish gain." I have considered the importance of this longest of all psalms right from verse 1–2. "Blessed are they whose ways are blameless, who walk according to the law of the Lord. Blessed are they who keep his statutes and seek him with all their heart." We must understand how important it is and why the Lord Almighty is requiring to give ears to his commandments.

4. "And keep all his statutes." Imagine you are driving your car on a dark night on a two-way traffic road without headlights. I do not need to say what will happen. I can see you shivering at this vision only. The statutes of the Lord are the light of our lives. Without them, we cannot see where we are going nor know what we are doing. Psalms 119:99 says, "I have more insight than all my teachers for I meditate on your statutes." Psalms 119:105 says, "Your word (statutes) is a lamp (headlight) to my feet and a light for my path."

The total fulfillment of God's promise for health and healing after deliverance from Egypt (the world) and salvation has always been and shall remain conditional. God means business, and there is no way around it. The story of King David, the man after God's own heart, or the entire story of Israel (people of God) teaches us that we should handle our salvation and our walk with the Lord with a lot of care, discipline, fear, and trembling.

The Healing Promise Fulfilled

The Bible declares the testimony of the Messiah as the spirit of prophecy. God revealed a unique prophecy to his servant Isaiah about seven centuries before Jesus came to a hopeless people who had fallen away from the ways of the Lord their God. Sin, all types of imaginable abominations, and more idolatry had led Israel astray. They had stirred up God's anger to the point where God had delivered them to their enemy. Beware of excessive disobedience. God himself will hand you over to satan to whip you a little bit and teach you a lesson before restoring you after your repentance and much crying. The people of Israel were in captivity again, this time in Babylon. Then, obviously, they cried to the Lord for seventy years. God spoke to his people through many of his prophets (Isaiah, Jeremiah, Daniel, and others) during that time period regarding their restoration and coming Messiah, Savior, and Redeemer who, without him, we can do nothing. Through the Prophet Isaiah, the Almighty Lord announced the Messiah many times. Then, one day, he declared, "The Spirit of the Lord God is upon me, because the Lord has anointed to preach good tidings to the meek. He has sent me to heal the broken hearted, to proclaim freedom for the captives and release from darkness for the prisoners. (Isa 61:1 KJV)."

He says again in Isa 53:5, "But he was wounded for our transgressions, he was bruised for our iniquities: the chastisement of our peace was upon him; and by his stripes, we are healed."

When Messiah began his earthly assignment, the first declaration he made to introduce himself to the world was that of Isa 61. He created such a controversy to a group of people, but great hope to others.

Blessed is he who comes in the name of the Lord, Yeshua Hamashiach of Nazareth, the Son of the Living God. He is the Alpha and Omega, the first and the last, the beginning and the end, the healer and savior of our lives. Things impossible to man (hearkening to the voice of God and obeying him) have been made possible by the blood of the Lamb of God. The impossible became possible because he is the Word of God that was in Egypt and in the wilderness with Israel, moving before them in the pillar of cloud by day and in the pillar of fire by night. He was the solution to the heat problem by day and the cold weather by night. The word of God that spoke to Moses and water gushing out of the rock for his thirsty children to drink was the solution to their hunger and thirst. He is the commander-in-chief of the army of God, who visited Joshua at the eve of Jericho's downfall. Christ, the anointed one, has now come to fulfill the prophecies. He is in Nazareth in the body of flesh.

> For the Word was made flesh so he could come and dwell in the midst of men. "He was in the world, and

though the world was made through Him, the world did not recognize him. He came to that which was his own, but his own did not receive Him. Yet to all who received Him, to those who believed in His name, he gave the right (power) to become children of God" (John 1:10–12).

This is the laying down of the foundation of the work of healing and deliverance of mankind, of which you and I are graciously partakers.

> Luke 4:16–21 says: He went to Nazareth, where he had been brought up, and on the Sabbath day he went into the synagogue, as was his custom. And he stood up to read. The scroll of the prophet Isaiah was handed to him. Unrolling it, he found the place where it is written: The Spirit of the Lord is on me, because he has anointed me to preach good news to the poor. He has sent me to proclaim freedom for the prisoners and recovery of sight for the blind, to release the oppressed, to proclaim the year of the Lord's favor. Then he rolled up the scroll, gave it back to the attendant and sat down. The eyes of everyone in the synagogue were fastened on him. And he began by saying to them, "Today this Scripture is fulfilled in your hearing."

Yeshua Hamashiach Is the Solution

I believe this Scripture is still fulfilled in your hearing and reading today. Yeshua the Messiah, the same yesterday and today and forever, is the solution to any health problem of mankind from the past to this day. He is the solution to any oppression, stress, anxiety, fear, and broken heart. He is the solution to any marriage problem, family discord, hatred, fight, war, and negative and bad thought. He is the solution to any consequences of sin in our lives because he nailed the sin of the whole world on the cross at Golgotha. He exposed the devil publicly, went to hell, and came back as a mighty victorious warrior with the keys of death and Hades in his hand. He holds the keys that he gives to whoever is willing to have them. Seek Jesus if you do not know him. Believe in what you have and who you are, and bind his word to your heart if you already know him as your Savior.

He came to set the captives free. He has been doing just that since that day in the Nazareth synagogue when he solemnly proclaimed that he is the awaited Savior. He is the one who the Father has sent, Isaiah 61:1, "to preach good tidings to the poor, ...to heal the brokenhearted, to proclaim liberty to the captives, and the opening of the prison to those who are bound." (NKJV). He has fulfilled a sacrificial mission for you just because he loves you. John 3:16 (KJV), says, "For God so love the world that He gave His only begotten Son, that whosoever believeth in him should not perish, but have everlasting life."

Believing in Yeshua the Messiah is complete without wavering or shaking. Trust in the Lord and veracity of the power of his word. In Ps 62:8, he says, "Trust in the Lord at all times, you peoples..." (NKJV)

> The Word of God is spirit and life. Hebrews 4:12–13 (KJV) says: For the Word of God is quick, and powerful, and sharper than any two- edged sword, piercing even the dividing asunder of soul and spirit, and of the joints and marrow, and is a discerner of the thoughts and intents of the heart. Neither is there any creature that is not manifest in His sight: But all things are naked and opened unto the eyes of Him with whom we have to do.

> The word of God created all things. He took the dust and made man, so he knows you. He knows me. Psalm 103:14 says, "He knows how we are formed; He remembers that we are dust." Because this divine truth is undeniable, the word has power to penetrate our body, joints, and marrow and destroy any strange presence, including cancer, ulcer, diabetes, spirit of heart attack, and all of them. In the name of Jesus,

they must obey and leave with trembling because the demons also believe. They tremble at the name of the Jesus. This is:[T]he Name that is above every name, that at the name of Jesus every knee should bow, in heaven and on earth and under the earth, and every tongue confess that Jesus Christ is Lord, to the glory of God the Father (Phil 2:9–11).

All the people who came to Jesus for help had health issues. There was so much sickness in the society (and there still is) that health or healing was the primary need of every living soul, especially the low-class society. The number of people Jesus healed during his earthly evangelization campaign is countless. These are just some few.

> Right after the sermon on the mountain of beatitude, Matt 8:1–3 recalls: When he came down from the mountainside, large crowds followed him. A man with leprosy came and knelt before him and said, "Lord, if you are willing, you can make me clean." Jesus reached out his hand and touched the man. "I am willing," he said. "Be clean!" Immediately he was cured of his leprosy.

> Matthew 8:14–17 says: When Jesus came into Peter's house, he saw Peter's mother-in-law lying in bed with a fever. He touched her hand and the fever left her, and she got up and began to wait on him. When evening came, many who were demon-possessed were brought to him, and he drove out the spirits with a word and healed all the sick. This was to fulfill what was spoken

through the prophet Isaiah: "He took up our infirmities and carried our diseases."

Mark 1:21–27 says: They went to Capernaum, and when the Sabbath came, Jesus went into the synagogue and began to teach. The people were amazed at his teaching, because he taught them as one who had authority, not as the teachers of the law. Just then a man in their synagogue who was possessed by an evil spirit cried out, "What do you want with us, Jesus of Nazareth? Have you come to destroy us? I know who you are—the Holy One of God." "Be quiet!" Said Jesus sternly. "Come out of him!" The evil spirit shook the man violently and came out of him with a shriek. The people were all so amazed that they asked each other, "What is this? A new teaching—and with authority! He even gives orders to evil spirits, and they obey him."

Mark 8:25 says, "Once more Jesus put his hands on the man's eyes. Then his eyes were opened, his sight was restored, and he saw everything clearly.

Mark 9:16–27 says:

Healing of a young boy with evil spirits of deaf and mute. "What are you arguing with them about?" He asked. A man in the crowd answered, "Teacher, I brought you my son, who is possessed by a spirit that has robbed him of speech. Whenever it seizes him, it throws him to the ground. He foams at the mouth, gnashes his teeth and becomes rigid. I asked your disciples to drive out the spirit, but they could not." "O unbelieving generation,"

Jesus replied, "how long shall I stay with you? How long shall I put up with you? Bring the boy to me." So they brought him. When the spirit saw Jesus it immediately threw the boy into a convulsion. He fell to the ground and rolled around, foaming at the mouth. Jesus asked the boy's father, "How long has he been like this?" "From the childhood," he answered. "It has often thrown him into fire or water to kill him.

But if you can do anything, take pity on us and help us." "If you can?" Said Jesus. "Everything is possible for him who believes." Immediately the boy's father exclaimed, "I do believe; help me overcome my unbelief!" When Jesus saw that a crowd was running to the scene, he rebuked the evil spirit. "You deaf and mute spirit," he said, "I command you, come out of him and never enter him again." The spirit shrieked, convulsed him violently and came out. The boy looked so much like a corpse that many said, "He's dead." But Jesus took him by the hand and lifted him to his feet, and he stood up.

You could just be in the presence of Jesus, believe in your healing, and receive it. A woman had nonstop, painful bleeding for twelve years. What a suffering she went through. When she heard Jesus was going to pass by her area, she went with all her pain, forcing her way through the crowd to reach out to Jesus with determination.

Always keep in mind that God will do for you or to you exactly what you want. Every situation we go through, whether good or bad, has its starting point in the mind-set. The following passage is awesome. Mark 5:25–34 (NKJV) says:

> Now a certain woman had a flow of blood for twelve years, and had suffered many things from many physicians. She had spent all that she had and was no better, but rather grew worse. When she heard about Jesus, she came behind him in the crowd and touch His garment. For she said, "If only I may touch His clothes, I shall be made well." Immediately the fountain of her blood was dried up, and she felt in her body that she was healed of the affliction. And Jesus immediately knowing in Himself that power had gone out of Him, turned around in the crowd and said, "Who touched my clothes?" But His disciples said to Him, "You see multitude thronging you and you say, "Who touched me?" And He looked around to see her who had done this thing. But the woman, fearing and trembling, knowing what had happened to her, came and fell down before Him and told Him the whole truth. And He said to her, "Daughter, your faith has made you well, go in peace, and be healed of your affliction."

We have read from Matt 8:16 that, in order to fulfill the prophetic scripture of Isa 61, Jesus healed all the sick. There is nobody who came to Jesus with hope and expectancy of great result and returned void or disappointed.

After his resurrection from the dead, just before he went to heaven to sit at the right hand of the Father, he handed over his power to the church. When Jesus gave his last and wonderful speech on the mountain of Olives (Acts 1:8), he transferred the commission of Isa 61 to us. We have received the spirit of power and responsibility to preach good news to the meek, heal the brokenhearted, and proclaim freedom for the captives and deliverance to them that are bound.

> Our forefathers, the apostles, fulfilled their part and even suffered tremendously for the spreading of the gospel. The Acts of the Apostles are a series of testimonies of divine healing power, deliverance from demonic strongholds and resurrections from the dead. In the early church, all who came to join were healed. All their hope and trust were exclusively based on divine healing power, and that is exactly what they received. Acts 5:14–16 (NKJV) says: And believers were increasingly added to the Lord, multitudes of both men and women, so that they brought the sick out into the streets and laid them on beds and couches, that at least the shadow of Peter passing by might fall on some of them. Also multitude gathered from the surrounding cities to Jerusalem, bringing sick people and those who were tormented by unclean spirits, and they were all healed.

Just like Christine Darg, who is crying out to the Lord in prayer and petition, expecting the restoration of the power and mighty move of the Holy Spirit in our churches today, let us humble to he who is faithful and pray for revival because we are in a state of emergency.

It is critical that the body of Christ begin to seek the face of the Lord very seriously. We should understand we are at the very end of the time and satan and his demonic government have kicked the children of God long enough. We should take a good stand to reverse attacks and demolish the stronghold according to the word of God.

God is faithful. If we seek Him with all our heart, we will certainly find him, and He will grant us His abundant favor. Jeremiah 29:13-14 states: "And you will seek Me and find Me, when you search for Me with all your heart. I will be found by you, says the Lord..." He will graciously let himself found by us and restore his Church as it was before. The days of old anointing shall flow again. He brought Israel back from captivity in consideration of his promise and faithfulness. A close study of Daniel, Ezra, Nehemiah, and ministry of Joshua (son of Jehozadak) reveals, at the end of Babylon captivity, the people of God led by these prophets and other leaders sought the Lord wholeheartedly. As a result, they did experience mighty answers. The God of Abraham, Isaac, and Jacob will do the same once more at this imminent end-time.

Let us all come together as one, putting aside every denominational barrier because we are one in the spirit of the Living God. The Lord promised the glory of the later house shall be greater than that of the former house. Let us join hands and rebuild the house.

I pray and hope these lines will generate a spiritual awareness and revival in your life as an individual, church, community, and nation, so, together, we will gather under a greater anointing and power to experience the glory of our Lord and Savior Jesus Christ with joy and awe.

Unto the Lord be the glory and honor and power, for he has done great things for men. He will do greater things for us when we believe and begin to work it out.

The Testimony of the Lord Yeshua Hamashiach

Acts 1:8 says, "But you shall receive power when the Holy Spirit has come upon you, and you shall be witnesses to Me in Jerusalem and in all Judea and Samaria, and to the end of the earth." (NKJV)

Holy Land Experience

The divine healing has always marveled me because we are serving an awesome God who always responds and acts beyond my expectation. He operates with signs and wonders, just as he promised the church he would do. Mark 16:17 says, "And these signs will accompany those who believe: In my name they will drive out demons; they will speak in new tongues."

Yeshua Hamashiach never ceased to perform miracles in the church. The great commission he gave his disciple on the Mount of Olives was to go and testify. Acts 1:8 (NKJV) says, "...And you shall be witnesses to me..." We must see restoration and/

or transformation of lives around us as we announce the good news of the Messiah's kingdom. According to a natural way of thinking, we should testify about things seen so the auditors of our testimonies may believe with confidence. That is what our social system calls eye witnessing, and that is what the limited human thought can apprehend.

God takes more pleasure in us when we believe without seeing. This does not mean that it is bad to see when we believe. We know Jesus Christ is alive, and we see the various miracles that he performs in our lives. The Lord commissioned the Apostle Paul to carry the gospel to the nations. He traveled from place to place, spreading the news. The Lord was confirming the message with miraculous signs. Those people believed without having seen Jesus. The same implies to me and to you today after two thousand years.

The apostles and other disciples who were with him had effective testimonies of what they had seen and touched. God confirmed their testimonies with miraculous signs and wonders. They were filled with the Holy Spirit and experienced astonishing health recovery as well as deliverance from demonic strongholds, death, and Hades.

It is extraordinary that, after two thousand years, the gospel continues to be spread. We also are believers today of what took place in Israel those days and have assured hope for everlasting life. Isn't it encouraging when we hear the Lord say in John 20:29, "Blessed are those who have not seen and yet have believed"?

However, believing the gospel without seeing involves an inner conviction, which is generated by the hovering and action of the Holy Spirit, the leader and conductor of the church of the Master Yeshua Hamashiach. This is what happens to us, who were not in Galilee or Jerusalem to see him in person, touch him, and hug him two thousand years ago. We were not there when he made the cripple walk, commanded the blind to recover his sight, or cleansed the leper. Believing without seeing involves God's grace by which we are saved and by which we also can experience the powerful transformation of our mind and body and become a new creation according to 2 Cor 5:17. "Therefore, if anyone is in Christ, he is a new creation; the old has gone, the new has come!"

When I was a young boy growing up in a small town in Africa, we used to attend church services every Sunday. I was sometimes acting in Christmas plays or just being part of various children activities in the neighborhood. Those activities, including Bible studies, really impacted our lives. In those days, we used to think the places mentioned in the Bible (Jerusalem and Israel) were hanging somewhere in heaven.

I realized those places were right here on Earth when I began to learn world history and geography in middle school. Even after I knew the Holy Land was right here on Earth, it had remained an overwhelming thought that God came into this world in the body of flesh and dwelt in the midst of men.

I had heard and read about the extraordinary stories of God's mighty acts performed in the days of old, leading his people from Egypt to Canaan. As an adult, I was still and always amazed at supernatural actions like those manifested with Elijah against the prophets of Baal on Mount Carmel and with Joshua and the downfall of Jericho. These encounters have marveled me to this day.

Before I take you over to my tour of Israel, I want to express the importance of God's grace in my relationship with the Savior Messiah. When I was saved in early September 1988, an incredible love for the Lord my deliverer burst into my entire being, a love that overwhelmed my soul. I had a warm and fine sensation in my spiritual being, like a sweet butterfly in my stomach. You can imagine something that makes you want to please and be pleased at all times. I could understand why the Psalms 34:1 says, "I will bless the Lord at all times; His praise shall continually be in my mouth." This fixation flows into your soul, which Yeshua alone is able to unfold.

As you grow in the Lord and with him, you understand that such a love is the mingling of two beautiful Scriptures that, together, are bound to create a spark that unites. It is a spark of everlasting fellowship. John 16:3 (NKJV) says, "For God so loved the world that He gave His only begotten Son, that whoever believes in Him should not perish but have everlasting life." God's love for us is beyond our imagination. So he helps us in our lowliness to fulfill his command, as stated in Matt 22:37 (NKJV). "You shall love the Lord your God with all your heart, with all your soul, and with all your mind." He who said "I am the Alpha and Omega" has done great things for us.

Since September 1988, I had the desire to see Israel one day. But that desire grew stronger while I was serving in Washington DC. Some churches I had fellowshipped with were organizing group trips every year. The Lord never let me go until the fullness of his time. Finally, I just said, "Thank you, Lord."

On March 14, 2008, our flight landed at Tel Aviv Airport. I had first flown from Washington DC to Brussels to join a group of eleven disciples from the Christian Brothers Community of Brussels (Belgium), led by my spiritual father, Apostle Jean R. Dipakayi.

The pastor of a local church in Tel Aviv Yafo, Pastor Tosh,

along with some members of the same congregation, came to meet our delegation and provide us with ride. We spent eight days visiting different places, just as I had dreamed to do for many years. No place we visited did not make me stand in awe.

Every minute of my stay in Israel, I was like in a dream. I kept saying, "I can't believe this is me in Israel."

Mount Tabor, the mountain of transfiguration, was the first location we visited. We spent hours praising and praying there, the place where Moses and Elijah came down to visit the commander of the host, King of kings, and Lord of lords. We made a stop at the Mount of Beatitudes. From there, we went to Capernaum, where we saw the house of Peter and entered the old synagogue where our Lord first healed the crippled man. We ended this first visit at the Jordan River, the baptism site, the exact place where John was baptizing and Yeshua came to him to be baptized. That was day one.

The second location was Jerusalem. Halleluiah!

We had believed and preached the gospel. But, today, I can tell you that, when you go there with expectation, you will never be able to describe your feelings. One member of our group, Mama Colette, had told me earlier, "You know, if you come here with expectation, you will receive it. But those who come just like tourists will go back as they came." Mama Colette knew my heart was full of expectation. We saw Golgotha. I went into the empty tomb, and I can testify, "Yes, the sepulcher Jesus was laid in is empty." Inside the tomb, I fell flat on my stomach. Behind me, a sister was lying flat on her stomach. Other brothers and sisters were there singing, "Even in the grave, Jesus is Lord."

The visit to the manger in Bethlehem was quick but awesome. This is where Herod, the King of Judea, sent soldiers to kill all babies, hoping it would stop the King of kings from fulfilling God's plan of salvation. That was day two.

The other days, we went to the Dead Sea at Ein Gedi. I was so excited to experience the power of the Dead Sea that I went prepared to lay on the water as if I were on a mattress. And I did. No living being can drown in there. Awesome!

We praised and prayed at the Western Wall in Jerusalem and later spent more time in the upper room where Ruach Kodesh came upon the church for the first time.

These are just a few of many places I was blessed and privileged to step in during my Holy Land experience. It is a blessing to believe without seeing. However, when I went there with expectation, it made a difference. Yeshua Hamashiach, the Son of the Living God, was made manifest to destroy the works of the devil. He died on the cross for the sin of the world and rose from the dead on the third day. He is sitting at the right hand of God, our Heavenly Father, and he is coming back anytime soon.

Written Testimonies of Divine Healings

For the past twenty years, I have seen hundreds of men, women, children, babies, and even those still in the mother's womb healed through the word of life and anointing of the Holy Spirit. Some of them wrote to testify to the glory of the Lord. I thank them for providing me with their written permission to document their extraordinary testimonies in this book.

Sister Naomi (Mimi) wrote:

This is the testimony of the divine healing power that the Lord has operated in my life through Pastor Jean-

Marie Sumo. One night in the year 1986, I went to bed as usual and fell asleep. Then I had a dream. In that dream, I had to attend a meeting in the cemetery with a bleeding chicken heart that I would hold in my hand. At the entrance of the cemetery, I saw a multitude of people who were waiting for me at one corner of the cemetery. All of them had a bleeding chicken heart in their hand. Before I got near to them so the meeting could begin, I saw my late senior sister, who had passed away a long time ago and stopped attending that meeting. She tried to stop me from entering the meeting, but I did not obey her. Rather, I ran away from her to attend the meeting. But she followed me, took hold of me, and brought me out of the cemetery. When I woke up, it was seven o'clock in the morning. I started having a heart problem that I never experienced before. None of my family members ever had heart problems.

I had to go from hospital to hospital, and they could not determine exactly what I had, but the doctors were saying I had a kind of heart problem they had not experienced before.

They did many x-rays, electrocardiogram, and scanners, and that was in vain because they could not see anything wrong. The pain was growing worse, and my condition became more and more miserable. Finally, I was disappointed because I had bags of medications that could not cure me, so I felt compelled to consult with the traditional doctors, who are witchcraft people, seeking for healing.

When I came to the United States, I thought I had found the solution because of the highest technology in medical sector.

From time to time, the pain was so severe that I would collapse. Those around me thought I was going to die. They took me to Washington Hospital Center directly to emergency. More than four doctors came and began to perform their knowledge upon me. But, unfortunately, the result of all their exams came to naught. Although they found nothing, they decided to undergo a heart surgery because they said I was showing signs of heart problems that they could not determine with the machines. They asked for my approval to operate on me. I declined their proposal, so they prescribed a bunch of medication. I could not go four hours without taking medication to calm down or kill the pain in my heart.

I met Pastor Sumo in November 1993 when he visited the United States, but, this time, I did not tell about my sufferings. He came back in July 1994. This time, I decided to ask for prayer, thinking: who knew why God brought him here, at such a time like this. One day, he came to visit me. While I was telling him about my problems, I passed out and knew nothing of what took place thereafter. I was told later that pastor had prayed on me and I was healed. As I was weak, I rested well that night and woke the following morning in good shape. The first day, I did not take any medication and did not feel bad either. The second day, I felt even better and so on to this day. A few weeks later, I trashed all the medication as a sign of my faith in permanent health that I enjoy to this day. I thank the Lord who heard my cry and sent his servant to deliver me.

Sister Vanessa. wrote:
I was given a business card to Pastor Sumo's church. I called the church and later visited. Pastor Sumo welcomed me to the church. I had multiple tumors, so the doctor told me. After that service when the man of God prayed for me, I went back to the doctor's office for final exams before any eventual operations. It happened that the tumors had disappeared. I believe prayer caused the tumors to disappear.

When V. came to the church that night, she was so scared that she could not even express herself. We prayed for everybody, as we usually did, without knowing she was under acute pain and pressure with uterine tumors. The following week, she came back with her children and gave the testimony of divine healing power with joy and awe.

Brother Emmanuel (Chicago) wrote: I have the pleasure to share this testimony with you so you know that God is always the same eternally. About three years ago, I had a dream in which the presence was manifested. I dreamed I was going somewhere. But, in order to proceed, I had to pass through a gate. A person was sitting at the entrance just at the time when I was going to pass the gate. I could not see the face of the person. He called me and said he was going to anoint me. I didn't resist to the offer, so I bowed before him, and he anointed me. He also anointed my firstborn son, who was walking with me at that time.

In August 1997, Pastor Sumo and his family came to our home in Chicago for a few days of vacation. As a man of God, the Holy Spirit spoke to his heart and told him to fast for three days. At the end of his fast, he told me the Holy Spirit had ordered him to anoint me. Without hesitation, I told him, "Let the will of God be done." He organized a prayer service at the house that evening, during which he proceeded to anoint me with special prayer. This took place on Friday, August 8, 1997, at 11:50 Pw.

On August 8, 1998, the Reverend Pastor Badette Gerson, who lives in Chicago, had a vision (dream). In his dream, he was evangelizing somewhere in Port-au-Prince, the capital city of Haiti. At that moment, a voice came down from heaven and spoke to him, "Gerson, see Brother Emmanuel is behind you." He turned around and said to me, "Oh! Brother Emmanuel, how come you saw me and did not call me?" Then the voice from heaven spoke to him again, "Emmanuel is prophet. Everything he says will come to pass." He turned to me and exclaimed, "Emmanuel, so you are a prophet and you never told me?" Then I answered, "Yes, I'm a prophet." The voice from heaven told him a third time, "Emmanuel has already been anointed to do the work that I have for him, which he has not yet started. Now he can begin the work without fear for I am with him and my power is with him." Then Pastor Gerson woke up.

He called me to relate the dream. We thought it was an ordinary dream like many others. But a month later, Pastor Sumo visited Chicago to accomplish an assignment God had given him in another community. He took that opportunity to come to my home one evening. His brother- in law, a young minister of Christ, accompanied him. After I had told him about Pastor Badette's dream, he stayed silent for a few seconds and then reminded me that the dream occurred the exact same date when the Lord commanded him to anoint me. The coincidence was so crystal clear that the pastor and minister went down on their knees to worship and glorify the Lord for using him to be part of such a sacred work. The most amazing part is that Pastor Sumo never knew and met Pastor Badette. But God, who searches the hearts, had used them for his works.

In 1992, Pastor Sumo prayed for my wife, who hadn't had menstruation for years. She was healed and began her period that same day, and it has been regular without pain. We bless the name of the Lord and pray he will continue to use this vessel to accomplish more sacred works for the well-being of humanity. May God Almighty bless you all. In Jesus Christ, my family and I are greeting you. Emmanuel Noisette.

I used to visit the Chicago brethren about once a year. We had regular prayer meetings in that great city, and our good Lord accompanied his mighty word with miraculous signs and wonders. Brother Manu is now a powerful instrument in the hand of God. The Lord is using him to touch the rulers of this world, bringing them to repentance and Christ. When I met Manu in 2003, he shared amazing missions he was undertaking through the grace and power of the Almighty God, among which he had a series of personal correspondence with Pope John Paul II, to whom Manu preached repentance and salvation only through Christ Jesus. The Lord anointed him to carry the gospel to many world leaders without fear or trembling. That is what our brother is doing. We thank God for Manu.

Sarah Norfleet wrote:
I would like to say, "Thank you, Jesus." I can now say that because I never really knew about Jesus until I came to 4809 Georgia Avenue and met Pastor Jean-Marie Sumo. I was so lost and hurt by not feeling loved. I loved everybody, but nobody really loved me until I came here to Jesus Christ Disciple Church, where I saw a church and pastor with so much concern for this area of town.

I was so sick from my addiction of alcohol and drugs that the doctors at the clinics had said I would not live six months. My kidneys were really bad, almost incontinent. My skin was yellow. My jaundiced eyes, yellow and red, were all swollen. I had high blood pressure. I was on medicine that made me so sick that I wanted to die from not knowing if I were coming or going. I was a zombie. I was dirty in appearance. I was dirty in my spirit so much that I only came to life at night for fear of the daylight. I was so ugly to look at.

This is what Pastor J.M. Sumo did for me. He prayed for me, and my addictions left. He didn't even know some of my illnesses. My liver and kidney were almost gone. He only knew I drank beer and sat at the bus stop with a bottle from time to time. I was so sick and swollen that I couldn't even walk across the street, and this made me want to die. All those doctors gave up. They didn't care after I couldn't stop drinking. But, when Pastor prayed for me that once, my drugs, alcohol, and street love all left because he showed me that I could be healed without medicine.

Pastor just said, "In the name of Jesus." The alcohol, high blood pressure, and stroke symptoms are all gone. I feel excellent. I now have perfect health. I can love and be loved, all for free. I thank God for Pastor Sumo because of his faith in his God and now my Lord, Jesus Christ, through whom all things are made possible and renewed. I must say that Doctor Jesus used Pastor's hand to hit my back and command me to stand straight, and I could walk up straight again. I never walked bent over anymore from back pain or shame. Now I hold my head high up and praise the Lord; I run up and down the steps of our church anytime I feel like it. I now have what I didn't know before, Jesus and perfect health. Pastor, thank you. May our Lord and Savior continue to give you healing power that only comes from God and faith in him. May God always bless you.

Sister Sarah wrote this letter on her first birthday in the body of Christ, her forty-seventh natural birthday. She was so damaged that everybody in the community was expecting her death at any time. She used to sit at the bus stop across the street, strolling up and down the area with other addicted men and women. She would behave like one who had lost her mind, but spoke good English (no slang) and had a smile like that of a naïve little girl. I sat near her at that bus stop a couple times, praying for her and inviting her to the Divine Healer. One day in September 1997, as I was ministering in Chicago, I received a call from the church. I was told that Sarah was in the church. "What is she doing?" I asked. They had had her wash and change clothes, and she was serving at the table. Halleluiah!

Sarah was baptized on December 1, and we moved her to our apartment. She was totally healed, restored, and saved. She served the Lord as a mighty intercessor, also helping with the children's ministry.

The Lord granted Sarah four more joyful and extremely happy years, and he called her into his glory in September 2001. Today, Sister Sarah is where we all would like to be. We shall see her there and praise and worship our dear Lord and Savior Jesus Christ again together. She used to ask me, "Pastor, you will write my testimony in your book, right?" And I would say, "God willing." Now it is done. I also thank God for Sister Sarah.

How God brought them together

The following divine healing operation is that of one devoted sister in Christ, who had tirelessly fought in prayers, seeking the face of the Lord, and crying out to God with all her heart for not only healing or deliverance, but more for assurance of salvation.

The Lord God orchestrated our meeting in such a mysterious way that any person would stand in awe when hearing the story.

Elizabeth Sumo wrote:
An Extraordinary Story

The healing and deliverance power operated in my life through Pastor Sumo's prayers is spectacular. I want to give a brief testimony, since my life story would be subject of a book. My story of experiencing the wonders of God began when I met the pastor in 1991, during his early days in ministry. I knew my trip to Douala was ordained, and that was where I found my healing.

I grew up in a large family in Cameroon, and I was living in fear, captive of bad treatment received from my uncles. They beat me and tried to kill me when I was seventeen years old. I suffered from severe headaches. As a result, I developed bitterness and hatred for my uncles, and I became very sad and rebellious. I ran away from my family and went to leave with the brethren in the church.

I was extremely independent and not submitted at all because of the rebellious spirit controlling my life. I met an evangelist, a lady from Nigeria, and began to walk with her, fasting and praying for deliverance. I then became captive of that lady. She took me away to a small, remote town to live with her and work for her gain. I lived there for about three years. I was in distress, spiritually and physically, and I was suffering from different sicknesses and spiritual disturbances. I was bound by wicked spirits not to prosper. I had graduated with a bachelor's degree, but I couldn't find a job. I got so involved with church activities that I became evangelist, traveling from place to place with this lady to preach and pray for people. I forgot my sufferings. My family had also rejected me because I was a believer of Jesus Christ.

I was a kind of evangelist without assurance. In reality, I was suffering extremely from bitterness, loneliness, sadness, and frustration. My faith was tossed and stumbling. One day, I got involved in a deadly car accident. Four people died in my sight, and I came out of it with a broken shoulder. I began to wonder about my situation, and I went about seeking God more and looking for deliverance. God answered my prayer the day I met Pastor Sumo, who was then in the beginning of his ministry.

The very first day I met Pastor, when he saw I was in pain with my right shoulder, he took my arm, straightened it, hit my shoulder slightly with his other hand, and said, "Receive your healing." I was made whole immediately. To this day, I never felt any pain. Glory be to God.

After that, he prayed for me, anointing me with oil. He broke the forces of darkness that had linked me to that lady, and he destroyed all those evil spirits that I mentioned above in Jesus' mighty name so I could now serve the Lord in the fullness of his peace and freedom.

I thank the Lord for the prayers through which God performed an incredible transformation of my life. He opened my eyes that I could once more acknowledge his love for me and be happy. A year later, he blessed me beyond measure to be his servant's spouse.

After two years, we realized I was suffering from a dangerous and awful barrenness. As a matter of fact, I miscarried many times. For months, I ended up with a false pregnancy, which was nothing but the presence of an impure spirit acting in me, and changing my entire morphology as if I were pregnant. The Lord revealed the spiritual therapeutics to his anointed as to how to undertake my deliverance.

The Lord told Pastor in a vision that my name had to be changed. The Lord Jesus is so loving and good. He took away all my maiden names and had me called "Elizabeth," showing Pastor that, like Elizabeth in Luke 1:13, I was being blessed: "And your wife Elizabeth will bear you a son."

The Lord delivered me from those barren spirits. Two months later, I was pregnant. The Lord blessed us with a beautiful and strong boy. At this time, we have three children full of Christ's life and wisdom. I thank God because it is all about miracles when I conceive. It is more miraculous to keep the pregnancies to their full terms and more miraculous victories against witchcraft powers before I can deliver. However, All the former names vanished with the curses they had managed over my life for years.

I thank God, who has graciously granted his servant the revelation of victorious combats in the spiritual realms. There have been a great number of healing and miracles performed in my life. I cannot count them for it would take to write a book to tell my story. I pray the Lord will increase more in Pastor's gifts and continue to make him a source of blessings for the people on earth. Amen.

A Blessed Encounter with the glory of God

How God Answered my Prayer

This encounter was not told in the previous release of this book. Many people who read it or heard about Elizabeth's story were eager to know about the revelation concerning a name change that became the trigger for her deliverance, healing and child bearing blessing.

In October 1994, she had been carrying a false pregnancy for four months. The medical checkups never diagnosed the problem, but the physicians kept saying that they could touch the baby, but no child could be seen in the sonogram X-Ray. After 13 months of "pregnancy", I watched my wife consistently and saw her sadness increase to the point of an early depression. One evening of July 1995, I told her that the Lord had placed on my heart to seek Him diligently. So I sought the Lord for understanding and solution, because I had concluded with full conviction that my wife was not or had never been pregnant. The question was to know what this kind of mysterious moving thing was, and how to get rid of it. What I received from the Holy Spirit was to retreat in fasting and prayer. I shut myself in the church office without bread and without water, and began to cry out to the Lord, asking Him for the key to unlock our bondage, because my wife and I are one in this distress. I had made plan to lock myself in that room twelve days, or until I receive an answer from the Lord God Almighty.

I prayed day and night, singing hymns and worshipping God, waiting for an answer. I said continually "Lord if you do not deliver your servant and my wife, I will not leave this room. Are you not the God of Abraham, Isaac and Jacob? Who made promises and they all came to pass? Are you not Faithful and True? Yes you are. You never failed. My belief shall never waiver, that you are the Alpha and the Omega, the Beginning and the End, the First and the Last. O Lord! My situation is before you, and it is less than a dot compared to the Red Sea that you divided asunder, and made your people of Israel walk in the midst of it as on a dry land. Who is like you O Lord, O Mighty Warrior, you made river gush out of rocks and flow in barren wilderness. O yes! my situation is absolutely nothing before you." And when I could no longer speak or carry my Bible to read, I called for my comforter for rescue, the Spirit of power to act and to groan within my being. I kept going for seven, eight and nine days. I began to barely utter words. Then I remembered David who earnestly sought the Lord until he spoke to his soul. This time I began to address my soul with broken heart:

> Bless the Lord, O my soul,
>   and all that is within me,
>   bless his holy name!
> [2] Bless the Lord, O my soul,
>   and forget not all his benefits,

³ who forgives all your iniquity,
   who heals all your diseases,
⁴ who redeems your life from the pit,
   who crowns you with steadfast love
and mercy,
⁵ who satisfies you with good things
   so that your youth is renewed like the
eagle's.
⁶ The Lord works righteousness
   and justice for all who are oppressed.
⁷ He made known his ways to Moses,
   his acts to the people of Israel.
⁸ The Lord is merciful and gracious,
   slow to anger and abounding in
steadfast love. (Psalm 103: 1-8, *ESV*).

I focused on God's faithfulness, love and compassion, "For God so loved the world . . . " (John 3:16). How can I neglect such a powerful statement? God has always confirmed His word with miraculous signs and wonders. Hebrews 2:3-4 says:

> ³ how shall we escape if we neglect so great a salvation, which at the first began to be spoken by the Lord, and was confirmed to us by those who heard *Him*,⁴ God also bearing witness both with signs and wonders, with various miracles, and gifts of the Holy Spirit, according to His own will?

I was in a position of expectation, with high eagerness to experience God bearing witness with miraculous signs and wonders. All my prayers and worship were based on God's faithfulness, God who gave me and my wife the same dream in many occasions, dreams in which we saw a family with children, precisely three. Truly, the Lord is the same, He never changed. He said "Hear, O Israel: The Lord our God, the Lord is one." (Deuteronomy 6:4).

The tenth day, I became extremely weak, since I could no longer fall asleep for more than two hours. An unusual anxiety began to attack my mind around 9:00 am, trying to force me to give up. Looking at the door, there was no key. I had made sure someone locked the door and left with the key. I would not give up. It was no longer possible to give up after ten days, lest Jesus died for us in vain. To the contrary, I launched a battle in the spirit, with continuous conviction that I possessed every spiritual weapons to destroy any manner of demonic attacks. For it is written:

> "For though we live in the world, we do not wage war as the world does. [4] The weapons we fight with are not the weapons of the world. On the contrary, they have divine power to demolish strongholds. [5] We demolish arguments and every pretension that sets itself up against the knowledge of God, and we take captive every thought to make it obedient to Christ." (2 Corinthians 10:3-5)

All negative thoughts contrary to the purpose of my consecration became captive by the Word of the Living God.

> "[19] Behold, I give you the authority to trample on serpents and scorpions, and over all the power of the

enemy, and nothing shall by any means hurt you" (Luke 10:19, *NKJV*).

Jesus gave this universal commission for His mission to be perfectly implemented on earth:

> "He gave them power *over* unclean spirits, to cast them out, and to heal all kinds of sickness and all kinds of disease." (Matthew 10:1, *NKJV*) . . . ⁸ Heal the sick, cleanse the lepers, raise the dead, cast out demons." (Matthew 10:8, *NKJV*).

> "For the word of God is quick, and powerful, and sharper than any two edged sword, piercing even to the dividing asunder of soul and spirit, and of the joints and marrow, and is a discerner of the thoughts and intents of the heart. (Hebrews 4:12 KJV)

This battle lasted about six hours. Around 3:00 pm a dark cloud hovered over the city of Washington DC, and thunder and lightning burst out of nowhere, windblows shaking doors and windows. I shook and shivered as though having a serious fever, and I passed out.

As I fell on the floor face up, I found myself snatched from the earth. I cannot explain or describe where I was. But in the spirit, I knew that I was far above the earth and could see the earth through the cloud. This vision lasted a twinkling of an eye. And looking down, I saw a beautiful Temple, with appearance like the Temple of Jerusalem, all built with gold. Then the vision carried me inside the Temple where I saw, still from far above, an old man in front of an altar, seemingly busy rendering service by the alter. All of a sudden, I heard a heavy powerful but soft voice emanating from the thunder. The voice said: ". . . Zacharias, for your prayer is heard; and your wife Elizabeth will bear you a son, . . . " Then I opened my eyes. I looked around me and toward the glass window. It was raining. This whole scenario seemed to have lasted seven seconds.

When I opened my eyes, the vision and the voice had invaded my entire being. I was paralyzed on the floor; and I said:

- Lord, I do not understand. My wife is not Elizabeth. You are an Omniscient and Awesome God. How can I understand this?

The same voice I had just heard from on high came straight into my heart:

- Your wife shall now be called Elizabeth. Go, change her name. Your son is called Elisha. . . He is my servant. Go, change her name.

- What about her last name? I asked. . .

The Lord did not answer. The place became so glorious and peaceful. The room was filled with a bright light different from the natural day light. But it faded away gradually giving way to the natural light. All of a sudden, I was strong, energetic and extremely happy for receiving the key from the will of God. I understood in my spirit, that she already had a last name: mine.

The Lord God appeared to Abram, changed his name to Abraham, and changed Sarai to Sarah. The Lord God changed Jacob to Israel. These changes of names were prerequisites of the mighty moves of God in the process leading to the mission of Christ and to our salvation.

I picked up the office telephone, called my wife and asked her to come meet me, for the Lord had spoken. I gave her a piece of paper on which I had written: "The Lord has blessed you. He has instructed me to have your name changed. From right now, your name is Elizabeth Sumo. That other name (that should not be pronounced again) was linked to the spiritual forces of wickedness in high places, managed by those who were after your life. They were after you because of Jesus. Now, you are blessed." The Lord had just given us victory.

I prayed for her as she burst in tears. That day was July 10, 1995. She became pregnant about sixty days later and bore me a son on July 10, 1996, just as the Lord had said.

Seek the Lord with all your heart

God is our Father, a loving Father who takes pleasure when we take time to seek Him. God expect us to draw near to Him, and He will draw near to us. James 4:8 says "⁸ Draw nigh to God, and he will draw nigh to you. . ." (*KJV*). The following passage of Jeremiah 29:11-14 is very significant in that sense:

> "¹¹ For I know the thoughts that I think toward you, says the Lord, thoughts of peace and not of evil, to give you a future and a hope. ¹² Then you will call upon Me and go and pray to Me, and I will listen to you. ¹³ And you will seek Me and find *Me,* when you search for Me with all your heart. ¹⁴ I will be found by you, says the Lord, and I will bring you back from your captivity; . . ." (*NKJV*)

The Lord placed on my heart to give just these testimonies

written by those involved and representing hundreds and more alike. I have always been amazed at God's miraculous signs and wonders that he faithfully performed to confirm his word. I will not cease to stand in awe before the glorious acts of God.

A Wonderful Visitation: My First Encounter with the Touch of God

I am a product of divine healing.
I have been privileged to experience the Lord's visitations a number of times. The first time he manifested his presence, his glory shone in my bedroom like an extremely bright fluorescent sun. He touched me softly on my shoulder while I was asleep and woke me up.

When I woke up, I was just asking who was there when I found myself flat on the floor with my face to the ground, covering myself with my hands. This took about three to five seconds. I was overwhelmed with fear and trembling. When I turned around to see what was going on, the light was gone. I stood up in haste, turned on the natural electric light, took my Bible with trembling hands, opened it at once, and began to read from Jeremiah 1. I kept reading until dawn. This took place about two weeks after I was saved and baptized in the Spirit of God. You can imagine that such a visitation after only two weeks in the Lord was a tremendous experience. I was completely in awe.

Right after this, I felt my body was totally different. I really became a new creation, not only in my mind, but more so in my body. I was stronger and in perfect shape. I just believed I was healed. The spirit of the Lord revealed Himself to my spirit. The Lord had changed my damaged lungs with brand-new ones. He had cleansed my stomach from ulcers and rebuilt all the muscles, bones, joints, and marrow in my body.

Six months later, I underwent a detailed medical checkup required for a job. The results proved all I have described to be true. To God be the glory. He has done great things for me and greater things he shall do for men. Yeshua my Lord brought me out of darkness and into his marvelous light. He gave me new eyes to see his glory. He renewed my strength and my youth. He continues to do this every morning.

This is the reason why, since then, my burning desire has always been and still is to see men, women, and children, young and old, being made whole through the will and power of God. I wrote the following poem to the Lord, to recognize His goodness. The goodness of the Lord is not only for me, but also for all those who can see themselves in this poem:

Salvation

When I found myself in darkness,
It was a time of loneliness
Seemingly that would never end.
Never knew someone bringing light
Would pull me from the deep dark night.
Deep breath, sighing at every bend.

Blindness had made its home,
Entangling every bit of thought;
Became natural companion.
What a life, what's the goal.
Oppressive and bitter fight
Crushing my soul to death,
As I keep diving to greater depth
While darkness said: "You are mine".

Amazing grace descending from
on high, took hold of my dying soul.
Just aware my divine visitor
Had pulled me out from bondage,
Setting me free from darkness,
I saw the glory of the Lord.

Exhortation

Thankfully, I had many occasions to preach or hold seminars on the subject of divine healing, but, most of the time, they were entitled "Restoration of God's People." I am going to present the answer to some of the questions I have been asked in order to exhort the reader who needs to know more of what to do in order to fully abide in the four conditions of Exodus 15:26.

> He said, "If you listen carefully to the Lord your God and do what is right in his eyes, if you pay attention to his commands and keep all his decrees, I will not bring on you any of the diseases I brought on the Egyptians, for I am the Lord, who heals you."

People have received the Lord Jesus Christ by many ways. Most of the people came to the church, attended a crusade, or any public gathering where they heard the good news, respondedto the altar call, and came forward to receive Christ through prayer.

Some undertook personal research to have the proof that Jesus is real and alive. They read the Bible and prayed to God to manifest his presence and power to them, and God did it. Then they found a church. Some were sick in hospital or prison when men and/or women of God passed by and prayed for them. Something dramatic took place in their life.

No matter which way brought you to Jesus, you did not choose him. He chose you, regardless of your personality, social class, lifestyle, or any physical condition. Everybody must end up as member of a local church, under a shepherd the Lord has placed there to teach and train his flock.

However, there is one thing that ought to be common to everybody in Christ. You must be born again. You must be born in the Holy Spirit. The experience of the new birth is indescribable. At the moment you are born again, all you know is that something extraordinary has happened. You feel in yourself that you are no longer the same person. A divine transformation takes place in your entire being. Your brain and mind are renewed. You begin to hate the bad things you were cherishing before. Bear in mind that you are a new creation. The Lord Jesus Christ explains clearly in John 3 (NKJV), "Most assuredly, I say to you, unless one is born of water and the Spirit, he cannot enter the Kingdom of God."

In order to have a good idea of how the new birth occurs, think of the physical or natural birth. When a baby is born, he leaves the world of the womb where his conception and formation took place for a number of months. Life in the womb is totally different from that of this world. The eating and breathing system are awesome. The baby's health and life are directly connected to the mother's own condition. When the birth takes place, he leaves the womb world for this physical world. Likewise, the new birth moves us from this physical world into the spiritual realm that we are effectively experiencing, that is, into the kingdom of God. Your love for the Lord and his word and your desire to be in the midst of the brethren will burst out, similar to what happens during childbirth. Many supernatural effects will become manifest. Among these effects, there should be bodily healing. The Red Sea crossing experience with total man restoration must take place. Whether it is immediately or gradually, a process of transformation has to begin right there. Romans 12:2 says, "And do not be conformed to this world. But be transformed by the renewing of you mind, that you may prove what is that good and acceptable perfect will of God." And the Lord himself will help you in your daily effort for renewal of mind.

If you have not had that direct immediate touch, then your pastor, church, intercessory group, or any experienced brothers can pray for your healing. Many believers in the church are demon-possessed and may not even know it. They love and serve the Lord, but they undergo spiritual disturbances, some at low level and others at high level. One brother wrote a book,

Demons in the Church, an outstanding piece of information about sicknesses and evil manifestations among members in the church.

We understand it is imperative to begin with committing one's life to Jesus and receive the Holy Spirit.

Draw near God and stay constantly in his presence. James 4:7–8 (NKJV) says, "Therefore submit to God. Resist the devil and he will flee from you. Draw near to God and He will draw near to you."

1 John 5:18 (NKJV) says, "We know that whoever is born of God does not sin; but he who has been born of God keeps himself,

and the wicked one does not touch him." Psalms 91:1 (NKJV) says, "He who dwells in the secret place of the Most High shall abide under the shadow of the Almighty."

To draw oneself near to the Lord demands a disciplined life, just like any enterprise we undertake with expectation of success. Discipline is required in studying the word of God and constant. Regular prayer is required to draw near and commune with him.

We have the spiritual strength to resist the devil by developing a fasting and prayer life. Set up a daily, weekly, and monthly schedule, and follow it strictly. Do not plan and fail to implement your own plan. Do not vow and fail to fulfill it. That is lack of integrity. The Holy Spirit will move with miraculous power when you keep a life of integrity toward God, men, and yourself.

Find a spiritual workout partner. Work out your salvation, including your health, with fasting, prayer, and request. The name of the Lord is like a strong tower. Count yourself among the righteous ones who have the grace and capability to run into the tower and be safe, knowing satan and his demonic strongholds of darkness were defeated two thousand years ago on the cross at Golgotha.

Demonic attacks begin in our mind. Do not let the thought attacks add up. They build up gradually to bring you to the level of stress, negativity, and moral depression. Bad thoughts will generate bad actions, even leading you to physical destruction.

Rebuke any beginning of pain sensation in your body in Jesus' name. If you feel a beginning of stomach pain, headache, backaches, and so forth, rebuke it, and claim you refuse it. By doing this regularly, it will become a part of your positive mind-set.

Commitment

It takes self-discipline to do what is required to maintain good health, and it is very easy to do the things that result in harm or lead the wrong ways. For example, we are more attracted by the kind of food and beverage that are sweet in the mouth but are not good for the body. "You are what you eat and drink." This goes as far as enjoying health and happiness.

It is very critical to make a commitment to take care of yourself. This demands exercise of your willpower and self-discipline because only you can take care of yourself. Make up your mind to follow the biblical principles of a healthy life and stand by those principles with steadfastness. The Bible, in its entirety, provides all the tools, advices and recommendations that, if well applied, will help you to be healthy and strong, soul, spirit, body and mind. Just consider the 9 components that form one fruit; the fruit of the Spirit. "[22]But the fruit of the Spirit is love, joy, peace, forbearance, kindness, goodness, faithfulness,[23] gentleness and self-control. Against such things there is no law (Galatians 5: 22-23).

The word of God is concluding with two wonderful passages.

Romans 12:1–2 (NKJV) says: I beseech you therefore, brethren, by the mercies of God that you present your bodies a living sacrifice, holy, acceptable to God, which is your reasonable service. And do not conform to this world, but be transformed by the renewing of your mind, that you may prove what is that good and acceptable and perfect will of God. First Corinthians 15:5 (NKJV) says, "Therefore, my beloved brethren, be steadfast unmovable, always abounding in the work of the Lord, knowing that your labor is not in vain in the Lord."

The grace of God, our Heavenly Father; the peace and joy of our Lord and Savior Yeshua the Messiah; and the communion and power of the Holy Spirit will always be with you. As you have come to the end of this material, I want you to know that this is a new beginning. Also know that I love you all in the name of Yeshua.

Amen.

About the Author

Dr. Jean-Marie Sumo is the organizer of Christ Disciple Mission Worldwide, a charitable organization that began its road mission in the District of Columbia with the purpose of uplifting the standard of life of the hurting people. Toward that goal, he developed his strong Free Food Distribution and Homeless Restoration Program. His outreach activities allowed him to serve as member of the Capital Area Food Bank Agency Advisory Panel for many years. After 14 years of operations in the nation's capital , God commanded him to relocate to Atlanta, GA and ordered his steps on the path of academic journey and achievement. He earned a Master of Theological Studies (from the Pentecostal Theological Seminary [PTS], Cleveland, Tennessee) and a Doctor of Philosophy Degree in Organizational Leadership (from Beulah Heights University, Atlanta, Georgia).

After serving two diplomatic missions in Africa, the British Embassy, and Consulate of the United States of America from 1985 to 1993, he left the secular world of business enterprises to respond to God's call as a Minister of the Gospel of Jesus Christ. He was ordained a Pastor in January 1994 before he finally settled with his wife in Washington DC in July that same year. Their lives and ministry have impacted many families in different parts of the United States and abroad. God has blessed them with three wonderful children, Elisha, Elizabeth and Jean-Marie Jr., all serving the Lord Jesus today with love and passion.

Dr. Sumo is a gifted preacher/teacher who has preached and taught numerous sermons, seminars, and workshops on the subject of faith, healing, and kingdom building in Africa, Europe, Canada, and the United States. He is considered to be an expert in the areas of spiritual development, which is demonstrated through his personal experience and testimonies. He's now passionate to teach religion and business at the university, while running Christ Disciple Mission Worldwide, for the Lord Jesus Christ's Kingdom.

Visit the Author's web site: www.cdmw.org
www.sumopublishers.com

Reference

Christine Darg, Miracles Among Muslims - The Jesus Visions

(Pescara, Italy: Destiny Image Jerusalem, 2006), page number (160)

Glossary

Yeshua: When the Son of God walked the earth 2000 years ago, His name was Yahoshua. It means "Salvation" or "he will save".

The name Yeshua was a popular variant of "Yahoshua". Many believers, especially Messianic Jews, strongly believe this to be His name. Ref. (What's in a name? Richard H. Harris III: Elijah's Cry).

I am well pleased to use Messiah original name in my book.

Hamashiach: The anointed one.

Ruach Kodesh: Holy Spirit is the name of the third person of the holy trinity.

www.ingramcontent.com/pod-product-compliance
Lightning Source LLC
Chambersburg PA
CBHW020310010526
44107CB00001B/53